The Teacher Boy

The Teacher Boy

*A Memoir of Life
in Eastern Nigeria*

Sylvester Uzoigwe Okereke

Foreword by
Chukwumerije Okereke

McFarland & Company, Inc., Publishers
Jefferson, North Carolina

LIBRARY OF CONGRESS CATALOGING-IN-PUBLICATION DATA

Names: Okereke, Sylvester Uzoigwe, 1937– author. | Okereke, Chukwumerije, writer of foreword.
Title: The teacher boy : a memoir of life in eastern Nigeria / Sylvester Uzoigwe Okereke ; foreword by Chukwumerije Okereke.
Description: Jefferson, North Carolina : McFarland & Company, Inc., Publishers, 2024 | Includes index.
Identifiers: LCCN 2024022839 | ISBN 9781476695662 (paperback : acid free paper) ∞ ISBN 9781476653464 (ebook)
Subjects: LCSH: Okereke, Sylvester Uzoigwe, 1937– | Teachers—Nigeria, Eastern—Biography. | Politicians—Nigeria, Eastern—Biography. | Igbo (African people)—Social life and customs. | Nigeria, Eastern—Biography. | Nigeria, Eastern—Colonization. | Nigeria, Eastern—History—20th century.
Classification: LCC DT515.77.O56 A3 2024 | DDC 966.94092—dc23
LC record available at https://lccn.loc.gov/2024022839

BRITISH LIBRARY CATALOGUING DATA ARE AVAILABLE

ISBN (print) 978-1-4766-9566-2
ISBN (ebook) 978-1-4766-5346-4

© 2024 Sylvester Uzoigwe Okereke. All rights reserved

No part of this book may be reproduced or transmitted in any form or by any means, electronic or mechanical, including photocopying or recording, or by any information storage and retrieval system, without permission in writing from the publisher.

Front cover images: *inset* The author during his days as divisional councilor, 1959; *background* St. Paul's Primary School, Okpanku (author's collection)

Printed in the United States of America

*McFarland & Company, Inc., Publishers
Box 611, Jefferson, North Carolina 28640
www.mcfarlandpub.com*

To my amazing wife, Patricia,
and my dear children,
Nneka, Gregory, Celestine, Chukwumerije,
Ifeyinwa, and Amuche,
for their extraordinary love for me

Acknowledgments

> ... it does not, therefore, depend on man's desire or effort, but on God's mercy.—
> Romans 9:16

My maximum gratitude goes to the almighty God, the Benevolent, the Magnificent, the Most Merciful and Awesome God for the gift of life and protection for my family.

I am highly indebted to my supportive, dear wife, the love of my life, Patricia Uzoigwe Okereke. Thank you for being there for me all these years. Thank you for being my anchor.

The idea to write my story came from my son, Prof. Chukwumerije Okereke, who, as an undergraduate in 1996, wrote a short, unpublished pamphlet of my life history, which he titled "The Living Legend." He encouraged me to pick up the project and cheered me on throughout. Thank you so much.

I want to thank all my children for providing for me and for making me proud in very many ways, especially for their support for this project. Thank you, Nneka, Gregory, Celestine, Chukwumerije, Ifeyinwa, and Amuche. You all are adorable, and I have come to know that your love for me knows no bounds.

······

Table of Contents

Acknowledgments   vi
Abara Okereke Family Genealogy   ix
Foreword by Chukwumerije Okereke   1
Introduction: The World at My Birth   11

1. Growing Up a Boy   15
2. The Festivals of My Childhood   26
3. British Conquerors Set Foot in Okpanku   32
4. Early Education   37
5. Travails in Boarding Homes   49
6. School or *Ijiegbe* Manhood Rite? My Dilemma   55
7. The Teacher Boy   65
8. And Death Broke Me into Pieces   73
9. A Politician at 21   84
10. My Three Terms as Divisional Councilor   94
11. Second Marriage   107
12. Sy de Moon Is Disengaged   116
13. My Time as a Farmer   124
14. The Nigerian-Biafran War   129
15. Back to School   137
16. Sojourn into Eze's Court and Customary Court   148

Table of Contents

17. My Philosophy of Life and Religion   161
18. Family Is Everything   171

Index   181

Abara Okereke Family Genealogy

ABARA OKEREKE

1st wife	2nd wife	3rd wife
M. Ukpai Njoku	M. Ivo Okorie	M. Ude Ngwoke

↓ → **OKEREKE ABARA**
↓

1st wife	2nd wife	3rd wife	4th wife
M. Elewe Uzoigwe	M. Ngwuta Ude	M. Udunwa Ivo Ude	M. Udunwa Onu Ngele

↓

B.

Sylvester Uzoigwe Okereke (m)	Louis Okereke (m)	Monica Okereke (f)	Paulina Okereke (f)	Victoria Okereke (f)

↓

M. Patricia Udu Uzoigwe

↓ **B.**

Nneka Okereke (f)	Gregory Okereke (m)	Celestine Okereke (m)	Chukwumerije Okereke (m)	Ifeyinwa Okereke (f)	Amuche Okereke (f)

. . . . . .

The author and his wife, Patricia Okereke.

Foreword

by Chukwumerije Okereke

On the night of September 11, 2001, I boarded a night KLM flight from Lagos, Nigeria, to Amsterdam. By the time we arrived at Schiphol airport in the morning, the news had come that the World Trade Center in New York had been hit while our flight was in the air.

If I'm being honest, I had no idea the magnitude of the event, nor was it a major concern to me. I had just arrived in the Netherlands to begin a one-year master's program on international environmental management jointly offered by Hogeschool Saxion in Deventer and University of Greenwich in the United Kingdom, with only 320 USD in my pocket, 30 percent of my school fees paid, and three months' accommodation paid in credit. This was all I had with which to build my life in a foreign country.

I did not speak any Dutch. I had never taken a flight before. My first flight (whether domestic or international) was the one I took from Lagos to Schiphol.

I was born in a very rural village in Old Eastern Nigeria in the late '70s. I played naked in the rain, swam, fetched and drank water from the brownish local river (Ivo River), went to school barefoot most of the time, studied under the *akparata* tree at the local school, hunted rats and rabbits with my age-mates (when dad was not at home), and sang with other children in the moonlight. The first time I saw a washing machine was when I arrived in Europe.

As I changed the 320 USD I had to euros and boarded a train from Schiphol to Deventer, my mind was occupied not by the attack

·······

Foreword by Chukwumerije Okereke

on the Twin Towers but by how I would build my life and studies on the little money I had and the steps I needed to take to translate my iron will into success.

Now fast-forward 23 years. I have a distinction in International Environmental Management (one of only two in my class) and a PhD, earned in two years and eight months (the second fastest in the University of Keele, UK). I have pastored a church; published four books, all with the prestigious Routledge; placed more than 80 academic papers and book chapters in top-tier journals; taught at the prestigious Universities of Oxford, East Anglia, Reading, and Bristol; trained several PhD students; been a visiting professor at the London School of Economics; led several high-profile international projects on climate change policy in Africa; played leading roles in many United Nations and global scientific assessment projects; delivered more than 300 keynote speeches; and been interviewed by leading media houses in the world, including BBC News, BBC World Service, France 24, China Global Television Network, Channels TV, Arise TV, and several others.

In the past year, I've published in the *New York Times*, assisted Nigeria in drafting a climate change law, and graduated from the United States Department of State's International Visitor Leadership Program on addressing the global climate crisis.

People frequently ask me what the secret to my success is, and my two-word response is, frequently, "My father!" OK. Perhaps this is an oversimplification, but it's difficult to overestimate my father's impact on my life. He was my primary mentor, inspiration, and motivator.

Deep Relationship and Bond with My Father

These days I hear people endlessly lamenting how little time they spent with their fathers or how little they knew their fathers. I knew my father. We were close as I grew up, and we are still very close today.

· · · · · ·

Foreword by Chukwumerije Okereke

Dad has six children. I am in the middle and the youngest of his three sons. I have always felt as if I was secretly dad's favorite child, although it is quite possible that each of us six children feels the same way. Dad has a way of making people feel special. He is an attentive listener with a knack for identifying what people are good at and a tendency to shower praise on them.

My father, Chief Sylvester Uzoigwe Okereke, was my dearest friend and constant company. I sat at his feet for several hours a day. I was always captivated by his intellect, wisdom, eloquence, and storytelling abilities, the manner in which he remembers facts, paints word pictures, and connects events with his tales.

When people lost loved ones, or when there was something to celebrate—say someone married, took a chieftaincy title, bought a new bicycle, laid the foundation of a new house, or survived an accident—or during the local festivals, the men would gather with friends and relatives to commiserate or celebrate. Often I was the one my dad would send to go carry the keg of palm wine and accompany him on such outings. During these conversations, Dad would frequently invite—and sometimes "force"—me to sit with the adults.

Our home is a rendezvous of sorts for the community. Most *umunna* (extended family or kindred) meetings are conducted at my father's house. Most major village meetings are held and most important community decisions are made in my home. My father's compound is also frequently the venue for settling family and village disputes. Dad was (and still is) the community's backbone. My dad is an honorable man. A remarkable man. He is honored and held in high esteem by the community.

My father occasionally invited me to sit in on these meetings and listen. Sometimes, I served the palm wine, pouring it from the keg into a rubber kettle and then into tumblers. Often, a man seeking my father's wisdom, guidance, counsel, or assistance on a subject would also bring a keg of palm wine, and my father would invite me to come and sit and serve or listen. These sit-ins gave me the opportunity to listen again and again to my father's many stories and adages.

· · · · · ·

Foreword by Chukwumerije Okereke

A Historian and Record Keeper

My dad is from a family of historians. His forebears were revered for documenting their lives, mostly orally through storytelling but a few in writing. My father inherited this trait and displayed it with flair and impact. He paired a natural talent for storytelling with systematic and methodical documentation of events. He is widely recognized as the keeper of my community's history, customs, and traditions.

In between the sitting room and his bedroom, he has a large room that could be called his library. The room has a small bed where my siblings and I slept before we were old enough to have our own rooms. In the middle of that room there is a large mahogany cupboard with several drawers. The drawers are filled with the diaries my dad has kept religiously since 1951. In addition to these diaries he also has hardcover notebooks that he used as journals to document different subjects. Some of the titles I have seen include: Okpanku history, traditions, and customs; Okpanku church history; notable events in Okpanku and environs; family events; events of the civil war; the history of missionary schools in Okpanku; and days as a judge in the customary court. There are many more.

Where there were any disputes or controversy about traditional rites or ceremonies, or if people wanted to know what happened in the past, they would come to my father for clarification. He would dash into his room and reappear moments later with one or two of his diaries and journals. He would open to a page and read from it. The matter would be instantly settled and people would be happy. At 86 years, he reads without eyeglasses, and his memory is still super sharp.

Dad loves to impress people with his knowledge of history. He talks repeatedly about his childhood. His father's love for education. How his father sought to instill in him the same love for education. How his father tried hard and in vain to make his cousins go to school and how the mantle fell on him as the first son of his father to fulfill his dad's aspiration of having one of his own go to school.

• • • • • •

Foreword by Chukwumerije Okereke

Father told stories about how he endured a lot of hardships at the hands of foster familes in faraway communities where he had to live to attend primary school. You see, his community was so rural and so remote that they had only Infant I up to Standard III. From Standard IV to VI, Dad had to live in neighboring communities in the home of other non-relatives to be able to go to school. His struggles while boarding in these distant communities, the influence of cultural practices on his decision to go to school, and how he conquered all these challenges are inspiring stories to read in this memoir.

Dad loves to hold his audience rapt with descriptions of intriguing Igbo cultural practices such as the horse-acquisition chieftaincy title, the cow ownership title, the manhood rites, the women-fattening room rites, and more. He loves to recount how he enthused his students and how he fell in love and married my mother. He tells stories of the Nigerian Civil War: how he was almost killed the day the Nigerian soldiers invaded our community as he returned from taking his younger brother for treatment in a hospital far away from our community.

In this captivating memoir, he tells stories about his days as a schoolteacher before the Nigerian Civil War broke out, about his experience and those of his family during the Nigerian–Biafran War, about his disengagements from teaching and politics and his achievements for his community. He tells of his days at St. Charles College, Onitsha, as a trainee teacher. How he was appointed the school disciplinarian on his first day at school. How he often went without food and trekked for kilometers on an empty stomach to do his teaching practice because he had no money.

One of his favorite stories and one that is vividly chronicled in this book is his foray into politics as a young man of 21. He has used this book to discuss the political structure at the time, the existence of what was known as county councils, native courts, district councils, and more. How he was elected unopposed as the first councilor for the division in his ward at age 21 in 1958. How he was elected again in 1961. How he won a third time against a formidable opposition in 1965. Dad loves to tell in detail how his third election was challenged in the court. He was the first person in all of what was then Awgu Division to have his election challenged in court at the time.

In this memoir, Dad recalls and narrates the conquering of the Igbo people by European colonialists, starting with the story of the Anglo-Aro War of 1901–1902. He explains the concept of warrant/paramount chiefs introduced by Britain as an indirect rule measure in Southern Nigeria, describing its origin, legal and political backings, and how they shaped the rural communities in Eastern Nigeria during colonial times. He recounts the establishment of schools and propagation of education and how the missionaries ran and managed the schools using what was then known as Assumed Local Contributions. Dad's oratory prowess means he was always the one or among the ones chosen to speak on behalf of the community, to negotiate with other communities (for example, in land disputes), or to communicate to the entire community important decisions reached by the council of elders.

Dad's Love for Education and Traveling

One of Dad's most outstanding traits is his love for Western education. He understood the transformative power that education holds, and he made it his mission to facilitate learning—not just for his children but for the entire community. My father was responsible for training many people in the village in school. He assisted several people by paying their school fees. Sometimes these people would give back in the form of farm work on his farms. Dad combined farming and teaching with amazing ease and efficiency.

Dad's father had three wives (Dad's mum and two other wives). Dad's father was the only male child of his parents. The reason he married three wives was so he could have more male children of his own. Dad's dad died when Dad was 17 and when many of the children (from the three wives) were still young, so he made sure he trained all the children in school up to Primary VI. This was at a time when many families were struggling to send one child to school. Dad has six children of his own, and with farm work and proceeds from elementary school teaching, he trained six of us up to secondary school and five through university—the first in the community.

But Dad was a man of many firsts. He was the first among his age-grade to attain Standard VI education, the first to be a teacher, the first to buy a bicycle (a great feat at the time), the first to build a house made of cement and corrugated roofing sheets, the first to be a catechist in the community's only Roman Catholic church, the first to own a patent medicine store, the first palace secretary to a traditional ruler, and the first to become a customary court judge.

His love for education led him to found the first primary school in my village. He donated a vast part of our family land so the school could be built. He cared for the school as he would care for a child—as if it were his own. After his training at St. Charles Teacher College, Onitsha, Dad was posted to teach at the school he founded before the Nigerian Civil War. He taught there for several years, and it was the highlight of his career.

One day the whole village was in an uproar. Children and adults alike were shouting and crying. Others stood dumbfounded, hands folded. This was the scene you would witness if someone died in the village or a great tragedy happened. But on this occasion there had not been a tragedy of that sort. No one had died. The sadness and this extreme reaction were because news had spread that my dad had been transferred from the village school to another school in the neighboring village of Amagu. Dad was disciplinarian for his house and the community. People brought him their stubborn children to discipline or used the mere threat of his involvement to induce compliance from such children. He exerted the same discipline on us, his own children. We were severely restricted on where we could go, whom we could visit, how long we could stay. Self-denial, he often says, is the price of greatness.

One of his most memorable experiences was when he traveled to the United States of America with my mother on the invitation of their first child, my older sister Nneka. In this book, he talks

• • • • • • •

about what he gained from this trip and why seeing the world was so important.

His Belief in Me and My Success

Dad believed in me, and it was this belief that helped me succeed on 320 USD when I relocated to The Netherlands for my master's degree program. From the time I was a child, his pet name for me was "doctor." When I grew up and asked him why he called me this unique pet name, he said it was because I was so clear I wanted to become a doctor. He transferred his love for education to me. My dad was one of the reasons I moved straight to get my PhD after my master's. There was no way I was going to let him down.

We often joke that my father may not have bile. Yes, he gets angry, but he is unable to hold grudges. His forgiveness is almost instant and effortless even when no apologies are offered. In 2015 some of his extended family conspired to take his palm plantation from him. The land belonged to my grandfather, but Dad converted the land into a palm plantation as elaborately discussed in this book. His brothers and sisters worked with him on the plantation, and he used the proceeds to train them in school. Now they wanted the plantation to be shared equally among the male children. Dad offered to let them have other pieces of land that belonged to their father, but they insisted that the land with the palms must also be divided. And when they took the matter to court, Dad chose instead to let them have the entire plantation. He didn't think it was right to resolve his family's issues in a court of law. And less than three months after this decision, Dad was freely relating with these brothers and helping them in several ways, not because they saw reason and asked for forgiveness because none did, but because that is Dad! Dad is a remarkable man in many ways. I know many people think their dads are outstanding, but I really think my dad is an outstanding man.

Foreword by Chukwumerije Okereke

His Philosophy and Proverbs

Dad has several proverbs and wise sayings attributed to him. He loves wisdom and the pursuit of wisdom. People often quote him when they are making speeches in the community. One such saying is that an ignorant person is worse than a blind man. Another one is that passing Elementary VI is not the same as passing in elementary sense. And another: it is laziness and not handwork that kills.

He loves family. He is a stickler for honesty and fairness. He loves community service. He often talks about the importance of courage, prudent planning, and tact in communication, about the need for integrity, the value of hard work, and the vital place of self-esteem and contentment. He often says that you can become whatever you want if you imbibe these virtues. Despite his achievements, Dad is a very humble man. He emphasizes the importance of practical charity. He lives his values and walks his talks. He believes that there is no tension between loving custom and embracing Christian religion, as readers will find in this book. Although he was the first Catholic catechist in the community, he is a deeply cultural man.

He loves truth. He does not mind standing for the truth even if he is standing alone. Father in many ways is a man of vision and a man ahead of his time, enacting the principle of inclusion and equality among his six children, both girls and boys. At a time when girls' education was scorned in my community, he sent his first child (a girl, Nneka Okereke) to a secondary school that was one of the most prestigious in the eastern region. Today she holds a Master's degree and is a senior social development specialist with the World Bank and making an impact in the lives of other young girls and women in my community. Dad also trained my two younger sisters in secondary schools, who today both hold double Master's degrees in various disciplines. He also supported my mum going to teacher training college, which had always been her dream, and eventually obtaining a National Certificate in Education and retiring as a deputy head teacher.

I am therefore indeed very elated to have read this book, which chronicles my dad's life, his truth, his beliefs and vision, and more so,

· · · · · ·

Foreword by Chukwumerije Okereke

to know that this book will be read by readers the world over and that those who read it will learn one or two things from the life of a boy teacher and remarkable community leader who grew up in the very rural community of Okpanku in southeast Nigeria.

Chukwumerije Okereke is Professor of Global Governance and Public Policy at the University of Bristol. Location at the time of writing: Oxford, UK

· · · · · ·

Introduction: The World at My Birth

In Nigeria, the 1930s were incredible times. To some, things were good; to others, those were the dark ages. But it depends on the way you look at it. It also depends on circumstances like the place of your birth, your childhood and what happened while you were growing up, or what formed the person you eventually became.

Take, for instance, those born during the period when the killing of twin babies was the culture in many parts of Eastern Nigeria in the late nineteenth century, even up to the twentieth century. These people had horrible experiences and stories to share. Some told of how they watched as babies were snatched from their mothers' breasts and how everyone heard the cries of these babies from a distance away as they were either being sacrificed or dumped in the community graveyard or *ajofia*, infamously referred to as "evil forest." In other parts, others told that a baby taken into the evil forest was covered with a clay pot and left to suffocate and die. Some mothers were rumored to have run off in the middle of the night to see if they could find their babies alive and at least breastfeed them. Others connived and had their babies—the ones found to still be alive—smuggled out to distant communities where they could survive and live.

Or consider those born into the slave trade era. In those times, brothers were wont to seize their own siblings and sell them off to slave merchants. Communities would also apprehend any one of their own believed to have committed one crime or the other and, in agreement, give them up to be sold into slavery and shipped off to

Introduction

Europe or God-knows-where. Such were the times. A person born in this period might, in telling their life story, have terrible experiences to share.

But there were also heartwarming stories, for it was also a time when people went about without a bother for the material things of life with which we now concern ourselves. Teenagers—boys and girls—cohabited almost in nudity without a bother as games were invented and played and adults hunted for game animals that were in abundance in the thick forests. In those days, folks traveled to distant lands to attend festivals and chieftaincy rites. And boys looked forward to their manhood rites, just as girls looked forward to the time spent in fattening rooms, when their bodies would be painted with *odo* and *uri*, while they counted the days, waiting to be sent forth to their husbands' homes.

In 1947, Nigeria witnessed a total eclipse of the sun. That day, in the middle of a sunny day, the heavens suddenly turned gray and, gradually, darkness descended on the earth. It was a terrible experience, for I witnessed it as a young boy growing up in the quiet village of Amaeze in Okpanku. It was an unprecedented event. No elder alive, back then, could say that they had experienced such a thing or that their forebears told them of such an experience. People ran helter-skelter. Goats bleated as if a knife were held to their throats. Women ran from the markets, calling to their children and husbands. Fathers ran home from their farms in fear. The world had ended, it was believed. The gods were consulted. Sacrifices were offered and rituals performed.

Not everyone understood science at the time. So, it took decades to finally get a grasp of what happened that day in 1947. That dark and memorable day became the measure of the dates people were born. It was common to find someone say that they were born the very year darkness covered the earth, or two years before, five years before, or a year after. So, when children were asked to provide details for their parents' obituaries, they gauged their parents' age using the stories they had been told about being born some years before or after the year darkness covered the earth.

······

The World at My Birth

I was born in 1937, 10 years before the year darkness covered the earth. But I am not among those who measure their ages or guess their dates of birth based on the total eclipse of 1947, for my birth was recorded by my uncle, Joseph Okereke. My father, Okereke Abara, named me after his wife's father, Uzoigwe. Years later, when I embraced the White man's education and religion, I took the name Sylvester at baptism.

I come from a family of historians; my forebears were revered for documenting their lives, primarily orally, through storytelling. I was born in the year Nnamdi Azikiwe returned from the Gold Coast, now the Republic of Ghana, after living there for three years. It was there that he founded a daily newspaper, the *African Morning Post*. On his return in 1937, he established the *West African Pilot* and became a trailblazer of Nigerian journalism and, eventually, politics. I mention this because the events that happened the year a man was born are significant to his life. That is why many—when they grow up—research what happened the year they were born. Some go as far as checking the date they were born against world history. The year I was born was also when the Second China-Japan War began. They would remain at war until 1945, when a bigger conflict—the Second World War—took over. And this is significant because the return of men who fought in this Second World War spurred radical changes in my community.

If one checked world history, one would find that it was in 1937 that the Walt Disney Company released its first full-length animated feature film. This film, *Snow White and the Seven Dwarfs*, is still celebrated and known all over the world today. But a boy like me, Sylvester Uzoigwe Okereke, born in the rural village of Amaeze in Okpanku, tucked away somewhere in the Igbo hinterlands, could not and would not know about such things as a film.

First off, there were no roads at the time. At best, the White missionaries who came occasionally used bicycles, and it was always a sight to behold. There were no electric poles, nothing to string wires or cables from, and therefore no communication whatsoever with the outside world. So it was impossible for a boy such as myself to know

・・・・・・

Introduction

anything about what was happening anywhere else in the world. But I knew what was happening around me and the events that shaped my life. It is this story that I now want to tell.

1

Growing Up a Boy

I was born on September 10, 1937, in the remote village of Amaeze in the Okpanku community, in the place now known and referred to as Aninri Local Government Area of Enugu State. In the early years, before and at the time of my birth, there was no local government or state administration in Nigeria as there is today. My people administered themselves through a council made up of every married male in the village and community. This council was headed by the oldest among them. They made decisions on all matters and events affecting the village and community at large, and performed priestly roles, leading their people through rituals, oaths, adjudications, and festivals.

European missionaries came into Okpanku and found that this somewhat democratic system was already in place. While kings and emirs ruled over the people in other parts of Nigeria they had conquered, the Igbo area had no singular ruler. The conquerors called the council of elders "old men," and the people—not understanding the tongue of the European conquerors—assumed that "old men" was "*udumali*." Therefore, the term *udumali* became associated with the leader of the elders council. Every village had an *udumali* who led them in meetings and in other activities. These leaders were then charged with reporting directly to the liaisons of the European missionaries and conquerors.

My father, Okereke Abara, was born to Abara Okereke and his wife Ukpai Njoku. Abara Okereke, my grandfather, was in turn the son of a man known as Okereke Obasi.* At the time, a powerful man such as my father was distinguished from the proletariats by how

---

*See Okereke Obasi family genealogy.

many wives he had, how rich his yam barn was, and how many titles he took. Title taking was an expensive, demanding, and time-consuming venture, modeled and structured in Igbo society at large to ensure that only the prominent and affluent could attain it. It was a way to structure the society in strata, such that one who took a title was higher up the ladder than another who had no title at all. The titles were also classified in ranks, such that after one title, a visionary and powerful man strived hard to take another higher in class and prominence than the ones he already had. Okereke Abara had taken such titles, so he was a man of class and honor. He had taken such titles as *Onyibe Ji** and *Mazi Inyinya*,† which was rare to find and costly to obtain at the time. The title rite associated with killing a horse was capital intensive and highly demanding, such that a man who was not affluent could go bankrupt after performing it. The person taking the title would provide assorted food

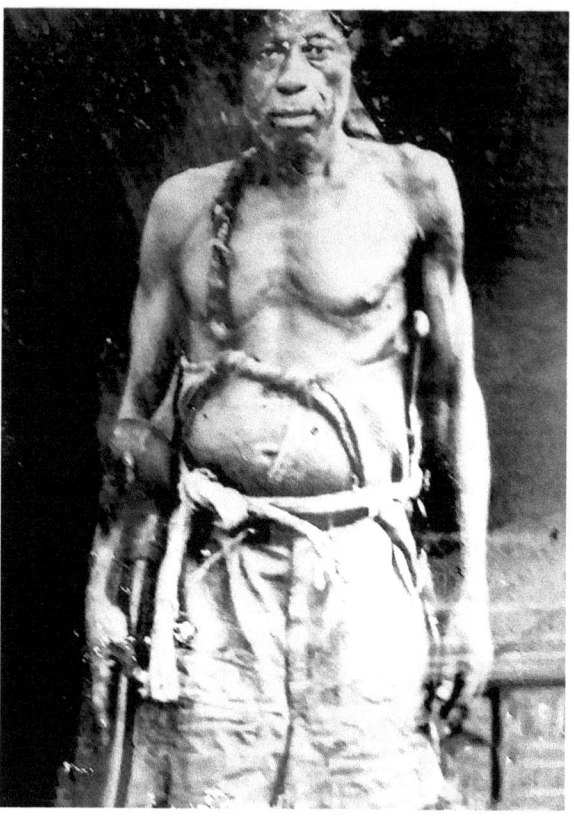

Mr. Okereke Abara, the author's father.

---

*A powerful title reserved for men whose prowess for yam farming was unrivaled.
†A title that shows he had purchased a horse and performed the associated rites.

1. Growing Up a Boy

such that his community and people from neighboring communities would not be able to finish what he provided within several days of merrymaking where assorted food and meats would be shared. He also took the Ogbu Evi* title.

Okereke Abara had four wives; my mother, Elewe Uzoigwe, was the first. She was followed by other wives: Ngwuta Ude, Udu nwa Ivo Ude, and Udu nwa Onu Ngele. These four women lived in the same compound as my father in the Umuogudu clan in Amaeze in Okpanku, each having her own hut for herself and her children. My father was a renowned farmer. His yam barn stretched from one end of the compound to the other, and yams were tied to barn stakes according to their sizes. But what distinguished him from his peers was that he was a prominent hunter. Okereke Abara was said to have been so successful in hunting that he killed two leopards and many other rare and daring wild animals, such that other hunters and indeed the entire community nicknamed him *Agulawu*. When I was growing up, the skulls of these leopards hung in his room. I remember standing before them—awed by their fiendish looks—and imagining how menacing the live leopards must have looked when my father faced them. He was indeed a huge and fearsome man to look at himself; he was a giant, with muscles and biceps such that one would think him to be a wrestler—and indeed he was one. His arms and legs were crisscrossed with arteries and veins, which were made prominent by hard work, trekking long distances to his farms, and climbing trees and treacherous valleys in the forests, where he ventured to hunt game.

Okereke Abara often ventured into the forests and lived there for days. Then, he returned with animals of all sizes, both small and big, that he had killed. This attracted many friends and villagers to our compound, where he provided palm wine and regaled everyone with stories of his hunting adventures in the forest.

He was also a known orator who held the community spellbound with his words of wisdom. He was so good with the use of words that he was a representative of Okpanku in dispute adjudications

---

*A title that involved killing cows for his people, second in rank to the horse title.

The Teacher Boy

with neighboring clans and the communities of Akaeze, Uburu, and Okposi. But my father's skills and bravery were not only nurtured by years of hard work; he was a chip off an old stone. He was, after all, a scion of a powerful man himself—Abara Okereke, my grandfather. Abara Okereke was feared throughout the length and breadth of Okpanku and in the neighboring clans and communities. He was a fearless warrior who distinguished himself during the intertribal and intercommunity wars of old. In wrestling, his exploits were the talk of the community for years. Stories are still told of his wrestling prowess, especially of how he got his nickname—*Dimgba*, meaning "great wrestler"—after he defeated a dreaded and famous wrestler from Akaeze in a wrestling contest. He was nicknamed *Avu Atu Egwu*, meaning "one who is dreaded."

My father's mother, Ukpai Njoku, was no ordinary woman herself. At the time, just as men fought and strived for recognition and prominence through sheer physical strength and wealth resulting from farm work, women did the same. And women were given the space to grow their own wealth through farm work and trading. As the men cultivated yams, considered a man's crop, women concerned themselves with the cultivation of cocoyams and, much later, cassava. Ukpai Njoku was hardworking and swift, so she became rich, prosperous, and famous, especially after she killed a massive river turtle called *Evemu*, which she caught in the Ivo River during the annual women's fishing festival, which took place during the dry season.

It was said that this river turtle was not a common one like the ones seen every other day, for it was far bigger and a hundred times larger in size; it would take several people to lift it out of the water if caught. Okpanku history records my grandmother as the first and last woman ever to catch this animal. In her lifetime, she took such titles as *Ogbu Evi*,* *Ogo Era*,† and *Oso Di Eme*.‡ And when she died,

---

*Women were also allowed to perform and take the cow-killing title if they were financially capable of it.
†A famous title conferred after a woman honored her mother by symbolically paying for the breastmilk she suckled as a child.
‡A woman who is as affluent as her husband.

1. Growing Up a Boy

she was buried with the highest honors accorded a woman who had achieved such feats as she had, using the *Ikpa*, which was a dirge dance, reserved for great people in Okpanku.

By my mother, Elewe Uzoigwe, Okereke Abara had five children, two sons and three daughters: Sylvester, Louis (who would become a high court judge), Monica, Paulina, and Victoria.*

* * *

My childhood was a roller coaster of intertwined activities. In those times, the world around us could be said to be innocent. Children, up to their teenage years, played in the village square or the markets—nude. No one cared about wearing any clothes. We played such games as swinging on a swing, which we formed ourselves on huge trees in the village square. Sometimes, we ventured into *Ajoali*.† Though it was regarded as an evil forest where evil persons were thrown away when they died or unknown corpses were buried, it also had fallow bush, which we used as ropes to form swings. Other times, we played in the sand. We inserted rings made from bush ropes into the sand, and whoever was the first to dip their hand through the sand and successfully extract the ring by finding its center won and was applauded by the others. We also played such games as *akpali* and *nkoro okpo* and engaged in swimming contests in the Ivo River to know who could dive better and who could swim the farthest.

In the evenings, Emmanuel Okorie, Hyacinth Okoro, Sylvanus Okorie, and I with others in our age group played in the moonlight. As soon as a particular group was heard shouting as they played in this or that compound or at the market or village square, others rushed out to join.

During our childhood, two dances were introduced to Okpanku. They were called *odabara* and *une*, and because my friends and I were experts in these dances, we made more friends: Fabian Ngwoke, Ugo Nwaja, Chukwu Nwa Okoro, Ivo Una, Ivo Eze, and Ogwo Chukwu.

---

*Refer to the family tree.
†The communal graveyard.

The Teacher Boy

Odabara is a special kind of dance with melodic beats that can wake one up even if one is in a deep slumber. The dance came from a nearby community of Okposi in present-day Ebonyi State. It was first performed at the burial of Mazi Obasi Ogwo of Umuchime in Amaeze Okpanku. After the dancers of *odabara* from Okposi made their scintillating performance to the delight of all of Okpanku, some young men and women from Amaeze organized themselves in a group and went to learn this dance from the Okposi people. The group that learned this dance was known as Igwebuike. They would become an age-grade in their latter years. My own age mates—people of my age group who played with me—and I named ourselves Obuoma Age-Grade. Not long after the dance came to Okpanku, we also learned it.

Odabara characterized and brought color to our childhood. We danced it from twilight until almost midnight. It was an opportunity to socialize and make new friends. Shortly after, another dance came from Akaeze.* It was called *une*, and both boys and girls could participate in this dance. After we learned how to play and dance *une*, we began to alternate the two dances. If *odabara* dance was performed on an Afor† weekday, then we performed *une* dance on the next Afor day. To ensure that the dancing troupes knew what dance was to be performed, the leaders notified everyone using a flag or a lamp. If what was to be performed at a particular Afor market day was *odabara*, then a flag would be hoisted at the village square. And if we saw a lamp lit at the village square, then we prepared to perform and dance *une*. It was an arrangement that suited everyone perfectly. Those were the best of times. I belonged to both dancing troupes.

Dancing to *odabara* and *une*, playing on sand, swimming in the river, and hunting for grasshoppers, grasscutters, rabbits, and fishes were our pastimes. We did not care about anything else. At that time, two boys who were our age mates, Alexander Aja and Michael Onu, were the only two boys who went to school. In the morning, they would leave for school, trekking some distance away to where the

---

*In present-day Ebonyi State.
†Igbo people have four market days, namely, Afor, Nkwo, Eke, and Orie market days.

1. *Growing Up a Boy*

Mrs. Elewe Okereke, the author's mother.

The Teacher Boy

school was located. We did not understand why their parents chose to send them off to school instead of allowing them to have fun with us. Of course, they shuffled to school reluctantly, especially after seeing us gather to make plans for what activity to engage in for the day. Little did I know that this was soon to be my lot.

During the daytime, we busied ourselves, making cuts on trees and collecting the myrrh gum. Then, we spread this gum on a long stick, stuck bait in it, and placed it on a tree. Afterwards, we tied a rope to the stick, held the rope to ensure the stick did not fall off, and hid close by. Soon enough, a bird would come to perch on the stick to feed on whatever bait was stuck to it, and its feet and wings would get glued to the stick. This was our cue to drag the rope and pull down the stick to catch the bird. It was a delicate operation that required special care and great patience.

Back then, the weather was much more mild, perhaps because the effects of climate change on the atmosphere were not yet being felt. First, the sun was not as harsh as it is today. Then, the rains did not fall as hard as they do in these modern times, and rainy season started earlier, usually in January or February. So, during the rainy season, we used hooks and ropes to fish at the stream and river, with millipedes or insects as lures.

Food was in abundance to a great extent. Our families cultivated mostly yams, *edu*,* *agbakara ede*, and maize. Cassava had just been introduced in 1936 by a Christian from the village of Amabiriba in Okpanku who worked with the European missionaries in Abiriba† and brought the cassava sticks from there. He was called John Onu.

Only the wealthy and affluent cultivated yams, so they were the only ones who had them in abundance and ate yams in their homes. When John Onu introduced cassava into Okpanku and the locals saw that cassava yielded a plentiful harvest, the Ohu titled men, a group of prominent and powerful men who had taken the *Ikeohu* chieftaincy title, reserved only for wealthy yam farmers, and ostracized John Onu

---

Edu is the local name for eddo, a starchy root vegetable that comes from the taro plant.
  Agbakara ede is a type of cocoyam similar in form to eddo.
†Present-day Abia State.

1. Growing Up a Boy

from the community. They claimed that he brought a crop that was going to eradicate yams; his action was considered an abomination. *Ikeohu* chieftaincy was a powerful rite, and only the affluent could fulfill the necessary rite and obligations required to obtain this chieftaincy title. Thus, the Ohu men were revered.

After the men cultivated their yams in mounds, the women planted *edu* and *ede* by the lower sides of the mounds. Children followed their parents to the farms and helped with farm work. Farming, in those days, was a pleasant experience, for yams were roasted and eaten on the farms.

Growing up, I relished waking in the morning to see that my father had returned from his hunting expedition. He often came back with game of various sizes, some still alive and others already killed. He always gave portions to my mother, his other wives, or his own mother, Ukpai Njoku, who was living with us, to reserve for food. The remainder was sold in Okpanku and neighboring communities.

I also had a nursing mother, who was my mother's sister. Her name was Ngagha Uzoigwe. I recall that she was the one who helped take care of me as a child. We lived in my mother's hut with Ngagha, my siblings, Ukpai Njoku, and Uncle Joseph. Dad slept on a mat on the floor. If a man had many wives, as my father did, then each of them would have a hut to herself. If he had just one wife, then the man and his wife and children would live in one hut. Huts were made of timber and sticks staked together and covered with red earth that was beaten into a clayey lump. They were round or rectangular houses built in the form of a big room; there were no other adjoining rooms. It was also in this single room that we kept our cooking tripod of three stones, clay pots for cooking, and clay plates for meals. Inside the same room was a "bed" made of mud called *ugbo*. The mud would be elevated two to three feet above the bare earth to form the bed, and atop it a raffia mat would be placed for the man of the house and his wife. The children and every other person in the family slept on mats on the floor. In the morning, they rolled up their mats and placed them by the corner of the room or on the bed.

· · · · · ·

The Teacher Boy

On top of the bed, the man could also build what was called an *ukoku*, a platform made with timber sticking out of the wall of the hut and covered with mud and a mat. The man of the house and his friends could climb on this to sit and chat. He could also keep any of his valuables on the *ukoku*. When a boy reached maturity and performed the *Ijiegbe* circumcision rites, he could build his own *ukoku* where he would sleep and invite his friends to visit and sit to chat with him or to spend the night with him. Most times, the boy who just became a man by performing the *Ijiegbe* could erect his own hut in his father's compound and build his own *ukoku* where his friends could come to stay and, most times, spend the night. It was not rare to see some sleep on the *ukoku* and others on the *ugbo*. So, if one who was still bedwetting slept on the *ukoku*, he could urinate at night on those sleeping on the *ugbo*.

When the boy got married, his friends would stop coming as his wife now stayed with him. The wife would sleep on the *ugbo*, and the man on his *ukoku*. It was an abomination for the woman to climb onto the *ukoku*. The children could have their own *ugbo* if the hut was big enough to accommodate more than one; otherwise they would sleep on their mats on the floor. All the children, both male and female, slept on the same mat. Boys could only climb onto the *ukoku* if they had become men by performing the *Ijiegbe*. Those were the days of innocence.

The hut was architecturally designed to have just one door in front of the house to serve as both entrance and exit. The idea for windows did not exist at the time. This absence of windows in ancient Igbo architecture could be the reason why, in the Igbo language today, there is no word for "window." But because the huts were made of clayey mud and finished with thatch roofs, it was mostly cold inside. Because of this, we made a fire inside the huts to keep warm on most nights.

During festive periods such as Aja, Omoha, and Ikeji, she took me to Ogbo Ugwo's* home, where we celebrated the festival with

---

*My maternal grandmother.

1. Growing Up a Boy

my maternal grandparents before returning home several days after.

By the late 1930s and 1940s when I was growing up, the European missionaries and conquerors had ended the intertribal wars between my community of Okpanku and the neighboring clans of Mpu, Uburu, and Akaeze. Consequently, these clans took a blood covenant to ensure that none would see or shed the other's blood ever again. The missionaries had helped put an end to child trafficking and slavery, so it was safe for us children to wander from village to village, forest to forest, and stream to river, playing and making merry, without a care for what was going on outside of the world where we lived.

. . . .

2

The Festivals of My Childhood

My community celebrated and revered three festivals: Aja, Omoha, and Ikeji. Aja Festival, which was celebrated around April or May, was one of the most prominent festivals in Okpanku. It was the period when women who were ready to be married were led into the fattening room after their circumcision.* They would be in a room, from morning until evening, day after day, doing nothing but eating and being taken care of by their mothers, aunts, and sisters. After their morning baths, *odo*† was used as cream on the bare bodies of these girls. Then, their bodies would be decorated with dyes called *uri*. In those days, the upper bodies of these girls were always uncovered; only their pubic area and buttocks were covered with a piece of material. But no one cared or noticed that the other was naked.

Aja Festival coincided with the culmination of many events in Okpanku, especially marriage rites. Before a marriage, a male suitor would give his intended bride gifts, which she was to show to her parents. If these gift items were not returned after four days, then the man would know that his intended's family was interested in seeing him come to make a proposition. And the first step in the marriage rite called *Inye Ive-l'eka* would commence. This is when he would come with palm wine in the company of his people to officially express their interest in his intended. After this would be the *Ikpa-olulu*, when the two families would gather to discuss the bride

---

*This is what is now known as female genital mutilation. It is no longer permitted or practiced in modern-day Okpanku.
†Camwood.

2. The Festivals of My Childhood

price to be paid by the groom's family. After this discussion, the groom would present some part of the agreed bride price, as much as he could afford on that very day; the rest could be paid later. The final rite, called *ibu-anu*, would follow afterwards. It was a ceremony where meat was shared for the families. If the bride were not yet pregnant, then the bushmeat provided for this ceremony would be shared among the families on a traditional chopping board called *okwa*. This is to signify to the general public, especially her would-be in-laws, that the bride is still a virgin. If she were already pregnant, then the bushmeat would be shared in a basket. Using a basket was both symbolic and a prayer for easy delivery for the bride, just as water easily flows out of a basket.

The day after *ibu-anu*, another rite—called *ibu-ulo*—would be observed. This is the send-forth ceremony for the bride, during which the bride's family endows her with household items for use in her husband's home. The quantity and quality of *ibu-ulo* items for a bride was what showed the economic class of her family. As a rule, *ibu-ulo* was only held on the final day of the Aja Festival. So, it was a big day for all eligible girls in the community who had already been in the fattening room for up to two months and whose marriage rites had been concluded, for it was when they would be sent to their husbands' homes amid fanfare. These brides were also welcomed into their husbands' homes with Dane guns being shot in the air by their husbands and lots of dancing and merrymaking. *Ibu-ulo* is still used in Okpanku as a marker to determine seniority in women's groups in each *Umunna*.* The *ibu-ulo* ceremony was also always celebrated on an Afor day. This special Afor day was called Afor Aja.

It was also during Aja Festival that boys were led into manhood in a rite called *Ijiegebe* or *Inwuegbe*. If a boy had reached the age of 12 or 13 or 14, depending on his maturity and family, especially when it was the time of his age-grade or group to be led into manhood, then his father would buy him a Dane gun and take him to the corner of the compound in the company of his older brothers and kinsmen.

---

*Kindred.

The Teacher Boy

There, he would be presented with the gun and a target—usually an egg was set for him—some short distance away. And the boy would aim at the egg and fire. If he hit the target, then everyone around would jubilate and pat him on the back, for he had taken the first step into becoming a man and was now ready to be led into manhood. If he missed the egg but the gun did not fall out of his hands, then he was also ready to be led into manhood.

If the gun fell out of his hands out of fear as he fired a shot, then he would be shamed whether he hit the target or not, and it was unlikely that he would hit the target if the gun fell out of his hands. The family would cover their faces in shame because it meant that the boy was not ready to be led into manhood and would not join the other boys of the same age. So, he would wait for the next Aja, the next year, to repeat the process.

News of a boy shooting the egg and the gun not falling out of his hands was usually announced with jubilation all over the village. The boy would then take possession of this gun and join other boys who had also successfully shot down eggs and, together, they would visit the homes of the girls in the fattening rooms. Like the girls, the boys moved in groups, from compound to compound and village to village, firing into the air and showing that they would soon become men.

On Afor Aja, just as the girls were being celebrated and escorted to their husbands' homes, the boys gathered at Afor Market to dance and show their prowess in handling their guns. Aja Festival was also an opportunity to thank God that during the nearly month-long period of young men handling guns and moving about with fanfare, no one had been injured. Before the festival ended, the group of boys who participated in *Ijiegbe* for that year would give themselves a name to distinguish them from other age groups or age-grades in the community. I observed *Ijiegbe* and was led into manhood with boys of my age group in 1951; we named ourselves the Obuoma Age-Grade.

It is important to note that if a boy shot at the target and missed, his family could not say that he hit the target. Back then, there was no need to tell lies or to be dishonest. Besides, the boy's family

● ● ● ● ● ●

2. The Festivals of My Childhood

The first five children of the author: Nneka, Gregory, Celestine, Chukwumerije, and Ifeyinwa.

and kinsmen would be present, so only accurate reports could be given.

Before my time, a boy who was ready to perform the *Ijiegbe* manhood rite was first circumcised. It was after the circumcision wound had healed that he was presented with his gun to kick-start the *Ijiegbe* rites.

After the successful ceremony of the *Ijiegbe* rite, held finally on Afor Aja, the boy would be considered a man who could marry or build an *ukoku* for himself. To be able to perform *Ijiegbe* and become a man, I risked dropping out of school. I will share this story soon.

Ikeji was another festival celebrated and revered in Okpanku to honor yam as the chief crop. It was held around August or September every year. This festival is known today as New Yam Festival.

Ichuaho was the festival held to mark the end of the year in Okpanku. During this festival, people came out to celebrate the end

The Teacher Boy

of the year. If a man had been accused of a crime or sin any time within the year, had been taken to a deity to swear to a ritual oath to prove his innocence, and made it to the time of Ichuaho without dying or meeting misfortune, he would celebrate and thank the gods for sparing his life and vindicating him in the process.

During Ichuaho, people came out, shooting cannons and guns and screaming, *"Aho laa oo!"**

If it was a fruitful year, then the people would pray to the gods that the coming year be just as fruitful and beneficial. But if it was a bad year, then they would scream, asking that the coming year not be as bad. And afterwards men would take drinks and gifts to their mothers-in-law.

In those times, there was no calendar to determine dates and pinpoint the exact day a year ended or another started. So, a man was assigned with the responsibility of monitoring the moon and alerting the community when it was the time for the year to end and for the new year to begin. For my community, Okpanku, the priest charged with this responsibility was a man named Chukwu Njoku. Shortly after our brother clan, Ishiagu, finished their Ichuaho, Chukwu Njoku would enter *Nso Njoku*† for a period covering seven Eke market days.‡

In the Igbo calendar, a week known as *Izu* and is made up of four days: Eke, Orie, Afor, and Nkwor. So, after Ishiagu performed their Ichuaho, Chukwu Njoku's people would announce that he had entered the period of *Nso Njoku*. Throughout this period, the custom forbade him from taking a trip outside his home. He could also not go to the farm or attend to any business at all. Instead, the villagers would visit to pay him homage, and he would present them with kola nuts.

Every night during *Nso Njoku*, the priest observed the sky, until he saw the new moon. It was after his announcement of this and the new year that Ichuaho could be performed. Chukwu Njoku's role and

---

*May the year end!
†A period of consecration.
‡Actually 28 days but counted as one month in the traditional Igbo calendar.

2. The Festivals of My Childhood

that of the priests before and after him can be aptly compared to the role of Ezeulu, the chief priest, in Chinua Achebe's classic novel *Arrow of God*.* Our people could eat fresh harvests from their farms only after Chukwu Njoku announced the new year.

When Chukwu Njoku sighted the new moon, he would beat the *ikoro* drum, and, on hearing the *ikoro*, everyone would know that he had sighted the new moon, and the celebrations would begin.

Omoha is another festival that shaped my childhood. It was a special festival for women, a period when women could earn or take on titles. This festival was usually performed by women in honor of their mothers. As a child, I looked forward to this festival immensely because the women would cook various meals, and there would be plenty to eat. During Omoha, women cooked special assorted meals to take to their mothers. Husbands also bought gifts for their mothers-in-law. It was a festival held after Aja, so it happened around May every year.

---

*In *Arrow of God*, Ezeulu observed the moon and, at the sighting of the new moon every month, ate one yam from the number contributed by the community. Then, he announced the new year the very month he ate the last yam.

∙ ∙ ∙ ∙ ∙ ∙

3

British Conquerors Set Foot in Okpanku

In 1901, British conquerors invaded Arochukwu. Before then, they had tried to penetrate the Igbo hinterlands but faced strong resistance from the Aro, who had formed a strong hegemony in the entire Igbo area, trading in all kinds of products, including slaves. The Aro had conquered the entire Igbo area and the areas now known as Equatorial Guinea and Southern Cameroon, forming what was referred to as the Aro Confederacy.

The Anglo-Aro War was fought between 1901 and 1902. And after the British conquered Aro in 1902, they began to penetrate the rest of the Igbo hinterlands. So, in 1907, British troops on their conquest mission headed by Dr. I. W. Hitchcock invaded Okpanku. The elders told of that day. According to them, gunshots were heard out of the blue, a kind that had never been heard before, and the community was surrounded. Houses were set ablaze, and local warriors and hunters who tried to put up a resistance were killed.

It was an unprovoked attack, and the killings and burning of houses were neither necessary nor warranted; the conquerors just wanted to put fear in the hearts of the locals. Having learned a lesson from the war with the Aro a few years previously, they no longer wanted negotiations or diplomacy. Their formula for conquering every community was to use force first and diplomacy later.

As houses burned and people ran helter-skelter at the sound of gunshots from the British troops, Okpanku people, confused about what was happening, packed up their property and prepared to relocate to new settlements. Then, an Aro man named Ukwu Owo who

. . . . . .

3. British Conquerors Set Foot in Okpanku

settled at Ishiagu surfaced. He informed Okpanku people that there was no need to abandon their homes and settlement, and that the White people who attacked them and set their houses ablaze had taken over their territories and were now in charge of the administration and leadership of their territory. Ukwu Owo also told them that the Europeans had become their lords and masters, and everyone was now answerable to them and not the council of elders.

The news was difficult to comprehend. Before then, Okpanku, like other Igbo areas, had no one single leader. Every village or community was administered by a council of elders, composed of married men, with the old men having the power and authority to make decisions. This council of elders was led by an elder known as *Onyeishi ali*. The British colonialists would later call the *Onyeishi ali* "old man," and the locals would corrupt this to *udumali*. Previously, an influential man, perhaps because of his wealth or because he was powerful in battles or wrestling, could control a certain village, his words could be seen as law, but he was no king or ruler. Everyone was king or ruler in his own household and answered to the village council.

So, it was difficult for the people of Okpanku and, indeed, the entire Igbo area, to comprehend that they were now under a single authority, led by a people they had neither seen nor heard about, a people whose skin color was different from theirs and who knew nothing about Okpanku's customs and traditions.

"How are they going to rule?" the people questioned.

Ukwu Owo informed the people of Okpanku that he had been appointed by the British colonialists as their paramount chief. He was to reign from where he lived in Ishiagu. His words were now law, and he would now serve as liaison between Okpanku and the British conquerors. So, everyone worked for and deferred to Ukwu Owo. Before he visited any village in Okpanku, he would send a dispatch to the *udumali* of that village, asking him to inform the people that he was visiting. Then, the village would ask a certain age-grade to travel about 12 miles—on foot—to Ishiagu to bring him. That age-grade would go with a stretcher, onto which Ukwu Owo would climb.

· · · · · ·

The Teacher Boy

Then, he would be lifted onto their brawny shoulders, and these men would carry him all the way from Ishiagu to the village he was to visit in Okpanku. When his assignment in that village was finished, the men would again carry him on their shoulders and trek back to Ishiagu. His feet were not to touch the ground, no matter what. He was indeed a lord.

Not too long after becoming paramount chief of Okpanku, Ukwu Owo relocated to Aliebo, a settlement in the Amaogudu village in Okpanku. He brought with him countless other Aro people, whose descendants still live in Okpanku to this day. When Ukwu Owo died, he was buried at Aliebo in Amaogudu.

Afterwards, the British colonial masters, led by Dr. I.W. Hitchcock and his team, selected men from each village in Okpanku to help their administration, in line with the Native Courts Proclamation of 1900. The aim was to use these courts to administer the customary laws of the land, which were formerly adjudicated by the council of elders of every village and community in Igboland. In 1901 a proclamation known as Law No. 25 of Southern Nigeria 1900–1901 specified that only legal cases that could not be resolved by the village heads or community elders were reported to the native courts.

The British colonialists selected men from every village and called them warrant chiefs. The warrant chief for Amabiriba, which is considered the oldest village in Okpanku, became the paramount chief or the chief of all the other warrant chiefs in the whole of Okpanku. He was the one authorized to represent Okpanku at the native court.

Those first appointed as warrant chiefs in Okpanku were:

1. Amabiriba village—Aja Ngwute
2. Amagu village—Uzoigwe Onya
3. Amaogudu village—Okoro Ngele
4. Amaeze village—Obasi Chioke
5. Okpu village—Chukwu Obi Mgbo
6. Ihuibe village—Chukwu Onuwa Onu
7. Uhuezeoke village—Eze Opanwa

. . . . . .

3. British Conquerors Set Foot in Okpanku

These men were empowered to rule as chiefs of their respective villages and in the native court. They worked with British political appointees who served as judges and clerks and some natives called *Kotuma*, whom most of them appointed themselves. The *Kotuma* served as court bailiffs and messengers and took on more roles, including acting as police, security at court, interpreters, and enforcers of the decisions of the court. They were so powerful that they could frustrate the natives who reported a matter to court or were summoned by the court. My father's experience in the hands of the *Kotuma* and the native court system spurred him to hunger for his relatives—and me—to acquire Western education, so that they would not be played as he was by the court bailiffs and their British masters.

In 1913, the paramount chief of Okpanku, Aja Ngwute, elected another set of elders to help him in his administration. They were:

1. Amabiriba village—Obasi Igwe
2. Amagu village—Ezima Udu
3. Amaogudu village—Chukwu Ogwo
4. Amaeze village—Aja Chioke
5. Okpu village—Oshi Ude
6. Ihuibe village—Aja Onunwa Onu
7. Uhuezeoke village—Ogbu Nwa Ngwu

No one knows why Paramount Chief Aja Ngwute developed an interest in education, but in 1928 he led some able-bodied men from his village to Uturu, a village in a place called Okigwe.* Those he went with were Francis Chukwu Nwaonye, Simon Aja, John Onu, Lazarus Ajamgborie, Romanus Aja, and Jeremiah Obasi. They went to a place called the Catholic Holy Ghost Congregation—the closest Catholic parish to Okpanku—to request that a school/church be established in Okpanku. This request was granted by the British missionaries, and, shortly afterwards, the Reverend Father Trech, of the Congregation of the Holy Spirit, was posted to Okpanku. Along with him came

---

*Present-day Abia State.

The Teacher Boy

Mr. Gabriel Chukwueze, an interpreter from the Ndeaboh community, who had been trained to understand the White man's tongue and language and to interpret it for the locals. With the arrival of the priest and his interpreter, the school/church took off in Aja Ngwute's court, with a celebration of the Holy Mass by the Reverend Father Trech. After Mass was said to bless the establishment and commit it into God's hands for the benefit of mankind, the school/church was named St. Paul's Catholic Church and School. It still stands in Okpanku today.

・・・・・・

4.

Early Education

My father, Okereke Abara, had a lot of love for education, just like Paramount Chief Aja Ngwute. The difference is that while Chief Aja Ngwute's motivation for education was unclear, my father's interest in education was driven by the need to ensure that those closely related to him did not suffer under the weight of lack of education. He could not be educated at the time as he was already elderly and a prominent hunter and farmer when education was brought to Okpanku, but he wanted his household to be educated.

When Western education first came into Okpanku, my father sent his cousin, Okereke Aja Nwaigbo; his half brother, Okereke Ogbonna—later baptized as Joseph Okereke; and his nephew, Abara Ugo, to school. It is remarkable that he did this in the face of the popular belief that only fools, lazy people, or ne'er-do-wells sought the White man's education. These relatives of ours did not fancy the White man's knowledge, however, and nothing my father did could impress on them the need for it. This worried and bothered my father so much that it was said that he would sit alone, despondent, brooding over their stubbornness and refusal to follow the path of knowledge.

At the time in Okpanku, schooling was not something most people cherished. Many fathers sent to school only those sons known to be lazy at the farm. This would change after the Second World War ended in September 1945 and the Okpanku men who fought in the war returned home with stories of their expedition in Europe and endless talks about the importance of education. In fact, they took it upon themselves to force every teenager in Okpanku into school.

· · · · · ·

The Teacher Boy

But there was resistance: Okpanku teenagers ran away into the bush every morning and hid until afternoon, after school had dismissed.

To ensure that there was massive school enrollment, these Second World War veterans from Okpanku formed themselves into a "task force" and moved from home to home to fish out those who refused to go to school and their parents. Their attention was mostly on the fathers of these school-age natives. When the task force entered a compound, most people hid in their barns or huts. Most laughably, some men hid inside their *ukoku*, thinking that the veterans would not dare climb into the revered *ukoku* of another man without a formal invitation by the owner of the home. But the veterans had seen war firsthand and developed thick skin for such things. They would boldly enter the hut and make a small fire in the fireplace. Then, they would sprinkle dry pepper into the fire and wait outside. By the time the room became stuffy, those hiding in their *ukoku* would come down as there was no other means of escape. I already noted that there were no windows or back doors in the houses built at the time.

As soon as the men climbed down from the *ukoku* when they could no longer bear the choking peppery gas in the room, they were tied up. Those seized were taken to the home of Sergeant Peter Aja, who was the leader of the ex-servicemen. They were beaten or fined until they agreed to send their children to school. In fact, most of the men, while they were in the *ukoku* under the intense choking heat of the pepper in the fire, would promise to send their wards to school if they were allowed to come down.

The veterans walked about the community dressed in their World War II camouflage and stomped as if they were going to war. They were revered and feared, and no one dared challenge them. They were seen as active soldiers who had fought a great war and could do the unthinkable. The teenagers whom they fished out were carried onto the school premises and shamed into going to school.

Before these soldiers left for the Second World War and men were being recruited to join the British expeditioners, my father asked Joseph Abara to join the expedition, but he said he would

······

4. Early Education

rather run away than go to war as he did not want to die. Only one Okpanku man died in the Second World War, however.

The Okpanku World War II veterans and their ranks are outlined below:

1. Peter Aja—Sergeant
2. Robert Okoro Aja—Sergeant
3. Ede Nwankwo—Sergeant
4. Daniel Igwe—Warrant Officer Class 1
5. Christopher Eze Oji—Private (Cook)
6. Aja Ivoke Eze—Lance Corporal 1
7. Nnaoka Chukwu Anyim—Private
8. Mathew Onyeze—Private (Bigler)
9. Aja Ude Obodo—Lance Corporal 1
10. Julius Okoro—Lance Corporal 1

Only Sergeant Ede Nwankwo from Amaeze died in the war. Also, he was not originally from Okpanku; his father was an Arochukwu man who settled in Okpanku.

Before the veterans returned from the Second World War, the school/church established by Chief Aja Ngwute and some early Christians in Okpanku—including Sir Aja Simon, John Onu, Francis Nwaonye, Paul Ivoke, George Uzoigwe, and Elias Aja—faced tremendous challenges from the locals.

Paramount Chief Aja Ngwute noticed the rebellion against the church and the school early enough. So, to ensure that the community would not burn down or destroy the church and school, he built the dwarf thatch house where the school/church took off in his own compound. As soon as the church and school began, resistance from the community intensified because the people believed that the values taught at the school/church went against their traditional beliefs and religion. Consequently, those early Christians suffered ex-communication from their close family members and the community.

Nevertheless, the school continued to grow with the help of the war veterans, and soon the thatch hut at the chief's home could no longer accommodate the school. Because the threats from the community made it impossible to obtain land for it from the community, the chief moved the school/church to land owned by his kinsmen in a place known as Oji. This land was donated by the late Ibe Nwa Makwe and Egbe Ogu, both from the Umuajali family. When the chief mentioned the need to expand the school and relocate it outside of his compound, his kinsmen told him that if he was not faint-hearted and could take his school to their land, which was being used as *ajofia*, he could use the land. Aja Ngwute accepted this offer, and the school was moved there. It would later be seen as a plus because the graveyard at Oji was central to every village in Okpanku. It was at this graveyard-turned-school at Oji that I attended Infant I and Infant II classes.

The early Christians came together to build a mud-thatch house and started Infant I and Infant II. The enrollment was poor, and there were no female pupils. Sending girls to school was considered a waste of time, as they were prepared from childhood only for marriage. When this school was moved to Oji, the headmaster was Mr. Vincent Uche from Agbaja.*

The first teacher and headmaster at St. Paul's was Mr. Gabriel Chukwu from Ndeaboh. Other pioneer teachers were Mr. G. U. Ochi from Ogugu and Mr. Michael Ude. The Methodist missionaries also followed in the line of the Catholics, and in 1936, through their converts—Job Ukpabi, Elijah Uzoigwe, Aaron Arum, Paul Ajaonu, and Peter Aja—they established their own school in the village of Ihuibe. The Reverend Okorocha from Arochukwu was pastor-in-charge of the Methodist church and school.

Paramount Chief Aja Ngwute faced great challenges from not just the locals but also his fellow warrant chiefs and elders, especially as Father Trech preached against idol worship and other cultural and religious practices of Okpanku. Only a few followed and supported him. It is not clear what motivated him, but whatever it was, it was a good decision that eventually brought civilization to Okpanku, years later. Thankfully, the intervention of the war veterans helped to grow

---

*Agbaja is now in Udi in present-day Enugu State.

4. Early Education

the population of the school. And as this happened, the population of the Methodist church dropped. The Methodists had to concentrate more on church services and winning converts into their ministry, and their school fizzled out.

With the growth in the population of the school and more people signifying interest, the ex-servicemen demanded that the community give land for the expansion of the new school. So, in 1947, a well-respected Christian and community leader, Francis Chukwu Nwonye, and his brothers donated their land at Aguta to the church, and a mud house was built by the community to accommodate five classes, a football field, a school latrine, and a two-room living quarters for the headmaster. Officially, St. Paul's Catholic Church and School was moved from Oji to Aguta in 1947. The Oji school site later became the host for the customary court, which still stands there today.

The site was found to be suitable as a permanent place for the school, and some people came together to begin negotiations with the landowners. They were the area councilor in charge of Okpanku, Councilor Jeremiah Obasi; the chairman and vice chairman of Uke Asaa Okpanku, which was a council of elders and the apex leadership structure of Okpanku, Okereke Chukwu, and Chukwu Ogbu; and the World War II veterans, represented by Daniel Igwe. Finally, on February 4, 1953, an agreement was reached between the landowners, the community, and the church, donating the land hosting the school in perpetuity to the Catholic Church. In the agreement, Okpanku was to provide the manpower that would build the church and school and to pay for enrollment of pupils, not exceeding 30 in a class. It was also agreed that the Roman Catholic Church would provide materials to build the school and then staff and equip it.

The men who donated the land and entered into the agreement were:

1. Onwukwe Onu Abara
2. Okoro Aja Elewe
3. Simon Aja

. . . . . .

The Teacher Boy

4. Dike Aja
5. Chief L.A. Ukpai

To help the people fulfill their financial obligations as stipulated in the contract, there was the introduction of what was known as Assumed Local Contributions (ALC). This meant that every adult had to be taxed to fund the school. So, Councilor Jeremiah Obasi and all the tax and rate collectors in the community decided to collect an agreed levy payable by every adult in Okpanku of taxpaying age to enable the community to pay auxiliary teachers in the Roman Catholic Church schools.

The divisional councilors believed that if the students were asked to collect this money from their parents, they would not return to school, but the tax agents and local councilors could do it, since they were respected and feared. This ALC was a special levy introduced into the tax regime so that when a taxable adult was paying

St. Paul's Primary School, Okpanku.
. . . . . .

4. Early Education

his tax and rate, he would add the ALC. This money was collected as part of the tax and sent to the divisional council. The priest of the Catholic church who oversaw the school was called the reverend manager. Father McGreen was the reverend manager at the time.

Hence, the church owned and managed the school, though it was under the supervision of the divisional councils. The money collected was first remitted to the divisional councils; ours was sent to Awgu Divisional Council. The divisional council deducted the ALCs sent in by the communities under it and remitted to the church. The Catholic Church, in turn, used this revenue to pay the auxiliary teachers under their employ.

Though the people owned the land on which the school was built and donated it to the missionary church, they also built the school as a community, while the church provided the zinc sheets and a carpenter to do the roofing. After this, the school became the property of the church. The church employed both certified and auxiliary teachers, paid the certified teachers from its own purse, and paid the auxiliary teachers with the remittances from the ALC. It can be said that there existed some sort of partnership between the natives, the church, and the government. This made the school function effectively.

On February 5, 1953, the community began the clearing of the church/school site according to the seniority of the villages in Okpanku. It proceeded from Amabiriba, the most senior village, to the youngest. And on May 12, 1953, the foundation stone for the church/school was laid by the Reverend Father McGreen. The building was completed on September 22, 1959.

My father, Okereke Abara, was not one of those who embraced education because of the influence of the missionaries or the World War II veterans. He did not send his relatives to school because he was forced to. Before the veterans returned in 1945, he had already sent his relatives to school. Even I was already in school, having been enrolled in 1943. My father's interest in education stemmed from

• • • • • •

The Teacher Boy

his fear that it would be difficult to get by without education in the changing world, especially in native courts.

His experience while trying to bring home the children of his late brother, Chukwu Abara, influenced this line of thought. After his brother died, his wife, Orieji Aro, who was an Ishiagu woman, relocated to her village and remarried without returning her bride price to our family. And my father, being the oldest of Abara Okereke's sons, fought hard for 12 years to get his brother's children back. His argument was that the children belonged to the Abara Okereke family and should not go with their mother to the family she married into or become her new husband's children. This case took him several times to the native court in Ishiagu and the police station in Afikpo, until he successfully brought back two of his brother's daughters, Orieji Abara and Ivo Chukwu Abara, to live with us at Okpanku. During the process, he was treated cruelly by the *Kotuma* and the administrators of the court, who took advantage of his illiteracy.

My father continuously said, "*Ife ndi ocha melu m, ajo ka.*"*

Indeed, the Whites treated him terribly, and he did not want anyone related to him to suffer the same fate. Years after my father passed, I took over his struggle for the repatriation of my remaining cousins, as it was my father's utmost wish, and I successfully brought back Maurice Chukwu on May 5, 1959, and Mgbo Chukwu on January 18, 1963.

In addition to Okereke Abara's travails within the corridors of the Ishiagu Native Court and the police stations, his earlier contact with the European missionaries, who were shrewd and cunning, and their Black agents, who were just like them, made him work hard to ensure that his own relatives were not as ignorant of the White man's tongue as he. Previously he was the village head of Amaeze and leader of the hunters' guild. He was a prominent man, so when he was not traveling to Ishiagu to attend the court case against his brother's wife, he would be representing the community in their land

---

*"What the Whites did to me was terrible."

4. Early Education

Mr. Okereke Abara, the author's father.

boundary disputes with neighboring communities. The most prominent of these is the Amaeze-Amagu-Agunkwo Land Disputes of 1944.

······

The Teacher Boy

To attend every court case in Ishiagu, Okereke Abara and his close friend, Makwe Akpa, would set off in the evening of the day preceding the hearing of the case. They would go through the forests all night hunting wild animals, which they sold when they arrived in Ishiagu. It was with the proceeds from such sales that they paid whatever was needed to prosecute their case. Sometimes, they trekked hundreds of miles to Ndeaboh or Afikpo or even the much longer journey to faraway Abakaliki for a land case. Once, my father and a man known as Ogwo Chuma trekked all the way to Awka* to get a surveyor to do a land map of the Agu-Nkwo area.† Today, the one and only land map of Agu-Nwko, jointly belonging to Amagu and Amaeze, is available because of my father's effort.

Traveling to prosecute those cases against Agu-Nkwo, Uburu, Okposi, and Akaeze communities as the village head of Amaeze made Okereke Abara a man who understood and appreciated the importance of knowledge and the White man's education. It is why he sent his relatives to school.

When Okereke Abara saw that his relatives were not serious about education, he sent me to school to start Infant I in 1943, barely six years after I was born, while many of my peers started Infant I at an older age. School readiness was assessed as follows: a child was asked to place his right arm across his head and see if his finger could touch his left ear. If it did, then the child had reached the recommended school age, but I never took this test.

* * *

When I was a young boy, my parents loved me immensely, and I knew it. They showed it in their attitude, words, and actions toward me. This fondness for me could be said to be because my father, Okereke Abara, was the only son of his father from his mother, Ukpai Njoku. In fact, each of my paternal grandfather's wives bore only one son. This was why my grandfather made my father marry Elewe Uzo,

---

*Present-day capital of Anambra State, approximately 80 miles from Okpanku.
†A portion of land covering about 23 square kilometers.

4. Early Education

my mother, early so he could have sons early enough. But my father would marry three more wives to get more sons.

Being the only son of his mother and having a son as his first child, my father had so much love for me. He also encouraged me to marry early, and in 1949, when I was 12 years old and in Standard IV, he got me betrothed to his friend's daughter, who was just nine years old at the time. It was this affection for me that made him send me to school. He believed that affording me the opportunity to learn the ways, language, and knowledge of the Europeans was the best gift he could give me. So, he did everything within his means to encourage me not to drop out like the others he sent before me.

My mother often gave me large chunks of meat to take to school as inducement. During school break time, I would bring out the meat and eat to the envy of the other children. Back then, no child went to school with food, not even water. Despite all they did to assure me of the value of education and the gifts I was given to take to school, going to school at such a young age was not something that I relished. I was barely six and missed playing with my friends at the village square or markets and traversing bushes and forests, hunting grasscutters and birds. I was afraid of getting flogged by the teachers, of the fights that happened often between schoolmates. We also had to fetch water for the teachers and help them get firewood. But my father, Okereke Abara, was several steps ahead of me. He sought out the teachers and gave them gifts of yams from his barn and game from his hunting. This made the teachers treat me differently, with kindness, such that even when I was late to school, as it was far from home, I was spared from flogging.

The war veterans began their campaign in 1945, when I was in Infant II. After the school was moved to Eguta, the distance I had to trek to get to school increased. Some of my friends—Njoku Uzoigwe and Ogwo Chukwu, for instance—dropped out of school at this time, and my predicament worsened.

My father would not even hear of me dropping out; he encouraged me as he did my uncles. And in 1946, I got enrolled into Standard I; St. Paul's Catholic School had added Standards I and II classes

・・・・・・

The Teacher Boy

at the time. In 1947, I finished Standard II at Aguta, and then came the next challenge. St. Paul's Catholic School stopped at Standard II. If I wanted to continue with my education, then I would need to attend school in another community, far from Okpanku, which had classes beyond Standard II. This challenge also caused more contemporaries of mine—Chukwu Nwaokoro Orji, Makwe Aja, and Mathew Aja—to drop out. Those who had dropped out were already enticing me to do the same. They had resumed dancing *odabara* and *une* at the village square and formed friendships with others, going for swimming, fishing, and hunting expeditions. It was an enticing life, and I was being lured by it.

. . . . . .

5

Travails in Boarding Homes

My going to school was a thing of great joy to my father, Okereke Abara. Not only did he now have a son who was willing to go to school, but this son was also doing exceptionally well. Each time I got home after the end of the term with my report sheet and my uncle Joseph Abara interpreted it for my father, he strutted about with pride.

One would occasionally catch my father pounding his chest with pride before his friends and contemporaries as he bragged about my academic prowess and performances. He always looked forward to the day I could be like the White man or challenge the White man. My father always believed that, one day, I would speak for him and become an important man in society. He always boasted that he was among the few who saw the importance of education and sent his wards to school without any inducement or duress. So, my father and his brothers greatly encouraged me not to drop out.

There was a great rivalry between the Catholics and the Methodists back then. If one was first indoctrinated into Christianity by the Roman Catholic missionaries, then it was akin to a taboo to switch to the Methodist church or to attend a Methodist church–owned school, and vice versa. The option left for me was to find a Catholic school with Standards III, IV, and V classes. Hence, it was decided that I would attend St. George's Catholic School in the Ndeaboh community, 10 miles away from Amaeze, for Standard III.

Ogbonna Azi, a palm wine tapper from the Mgbowo community,

······

used to come tap wine from the trees in Okpanku. He was my father's close friend, and his family lived in Ndeaboh. My father often bought palm wine from him, and he always bought bushmeat from my father. Occasionally, he visited our home to converse with my father, and they shared a keg of palm wine. On one of those visits, my father told him of the situation and requested that his family at Ndeaboh accommodate me, so I could attend school at St. George's Catholic School. Ogbonna Azi agreed. He also promised my father that his wife would accommodate me and care for me.

One Sunday, we set out for Ndeaboh. After all was set, my father took me on a bicycle and in the company of Ogbonna Azi. Thus, I went to live with Ogbonna Azi's family at Ndeaboh. Before we set out, my mother packed some cooked and uncooked food items for me. It was the first time I would leave my family for that long, and I dreaded going to live in such a faraway place. I was going to miss my mother and the meat my father brought from his hunting outings. I was going to miss my friends and all the activities we engaged in daily after school at St. Paul's. I cried and cried, but they did not pay any attention to my pleas to be allowed to stay back. My father already had his eyes set on the future. He was certain that education was the only means to navigate the ever-changing world, not the physical strength required to fight leopards in the bush like he did or wrestle strong men like his father did, not even the proficient use of words of wisdom at land disputes that he was known for. He knew that it would soon be impossible for men like him without education to get by, and he did not want his family to be left behind. His relatives, especially Joseph Abara, had already disappointed him by dropping out; he did not want me to do so too.

Before we left, while I cried and bemoaned what my fate might become at Ndeaboh, my father called me, and we had a conversation.

He said to me, "My son, I know what the value of education is, though I did not go to school myself. I strived hard to send my brothers to school. I also sent the sons of my sisters to school, but they all dropped out. I could not do anything to them because they are not my blood children." Then he asked, "Now, you who are my son, if you

· · · · · ·

5. Travails in Boarding Homes

refuse to go to school, if you refuse to do what your father wants and disobey him, as you now want to do by refusing to go to school, who will become your father?"

It was a difficult question, one that no right-thinking child had easy answer to. My tongue clung to the roof of my dry mouth as I stared at the ground, not knowing what to say to him.

"They have all disobeyed me," he continued. "They dropped out of school and wasted all my money and efforts. What will I do to them? Will I say that I am no longer their father? I cannot because they are not my own blood sons like you," he said. "But, if you, my son, disobey me, I ask you, who will be your father?"

After this conversation, I agreed to leave for Ndeaboh.

We arrived in Ndeaboh before noon. Mr. Ogbonna Azi introduced me to his wife and family and to other pupils attending St. George Catholic School. He asked them to take me to the school the next day being Monday and instructed them to make sure they escorted me back from school at dismissal. Two of the boys he introduced to me that afternoon happened to be in the same class as I was, so we became friends instantly; they are Onuoha Dibia and Ejiaka Azionu. At school, I was delighted to meet other boys from Okpanku (but not from my village of Amaeze) who were my seniors, like Andrew Uzoigwe from Amagu-Okpanku and Luke Uche from Okpu-Okpanku.

Less than three weeks after I began to live with Ogbonna Azi's family, his wife told me that all the food I had brought was gone.

"All of it?" I inquired.

"Yes. All of it. You must send word to your family to bring more food."

This was a surprise to me since I was sure that the foodstuffs my mother and father had given me could last for a long time. But the woman began to send me out to school hungry. Most times, even when I returned from school in the afternoon, there would be no food to eat. And when I returned from school, I was required to go fetch water from the village well, a journey of over two miles from their home. By the time I got to the well and queued to fetch water, it

· · · · · ·

The Teacher Boy

would be around eight o'clock at night. Yet, in the morning, Ogbonna Azi's wife would hand me just a cup of water to wash my face before I went to school. I would not bathe.

No matter how frequently my father brought food—he brought foodstuffs every time he passed through Ndeaboh on his way to represent my village in a land dispute with Amagu people—the woman would soon inform me that my food was gone. She also always marked the water level in her waterpot with chalk, to be sure that I did not so much as take a cup of water from the pot.

On Saturdays and Sundays, she made me follow her to the farm and work until late in the evening, leaving me with no time to do my homework. I worked for her at home and on her farm—on an empty stomach most of the time. This made school difficult for me. Because her husband lived at Okpanku, he did not know what I was enduring at the hands of his wife.

I complained to my father about this, repeatedly, each time he stopped by on his journey to drop off foodstuffs for me. By this time, I was already lean, and my stomach concave like a lizard's. My father was worried but did not want me to quit, so after the first term of Standard III at St. George, I was moved to another home at a village called Azu-nkwo Mgbowo in Ndeaboh. This time, I lived with a woman named Ngwute Mgborie, who was from the village of Amabiriba in Okpanku but married to Mr. Alfred Chukwu from Mgbowo. I was relieved because Azu-nkwo was close to my school, but my condition did not improve in the least. In fact, it degenerated, and I soon saw that I had gone from the frying pan into the fire.

Ngwute Mgborie was not only meaner than the first woman I lived with; her attitude and strictness were triple strength. It is difficult to document what I suffered at her hands. Just like the first woman, she also marked the water level in the waterpot with chalk in the hut without my knowledge. Whenever she returned, she checked to see if the water level went lower than the mark.

The first thing she would say was "Uzoigwe!" and my heart would sink into my stomach.

"Whom did you bring from school to drink my water?"

· · · · · ·

5. Travails in Boarding Homes

I would reply that there was no one. Of course, water was scarce, and I never brought anyone home to drink water. I may have taken a cup to quench my own thirst, but she would beat me mercilessly. She would then order me to go in search of water, no matter the time of the day, at a place known as Ogbo Mbara at Umurah Ndeaboh, about five miles away.

Her favorite dish was soup made with *akpakoro*.* What I did not know was that the woman counted the number of *akpakoro* she put in the soup. After eating and when I left for school, she also counted the remainder. And when I returned from school and she from the farm, she again counted the *akpakoro* in the soup to be sure that I had not pilfered any. Counting the *akpakoro* in her soup was the first thing she did whenever she returned from the farm. Before going to school, I could count on my fingers the few boluses of fufu I ate. Ngwute Mgborie also hated to see me come to the house with my peers, including my schoolmates. She believed that with them I might finish the food in the house or drink from her waterpot.

My father, having learned from my experience while living with Ogbonna Azi's wife, made sure that he brought me food every two weeks, rather than at up to three-week intervals as he had before. He always brought foodstuffs and pocket money to make sure I did not starve at school. My mother missed me dearly. She had also heard of my travails, so she sometimes braved the long journey of 10 miles from Okpanku to Ndeaboh on foot to bring me cooked food.

Besides school, students were also enrolled in catechism classes. So, in 1948, in the second term of my Standard III, I was baptized as a Roman Catholic by the Reverend Father McGreen, and I took the name Sylvester. I also received the sacrament of confirmation the same year with the name Reuben.

Again, more students dropped out of school because of the distance and because they were facing situations similar to mine. When I finished Standard III and it was time for Standard IV, there was need to move again. My school in Ndeaboh did have a Standard

---

*Water snail.

The Teacher Boy

IV class, but because of the wickedness and stress I was being put through, I needed to go elsewhere.

A school at Uburu* had Standard IV. It was also named St. Paul's Catholic School. Since Uburu was closer to Okpanku than Ndeaboh, I decided to relocate to Uburu, encouraged by one Emmanuel Okorie. Some of my schoolmates who relocated with me were Sylvanus Okorie, Mathias Uzoigwe, Tobias Enebe, and Thomas Oti. Together, we attended Standard IV and V classes at St. Paul's Catholic School, Uburu.

---

*Present-day Ebonyi State.

・・・・・・

6

School or *Ijiegbe* Manhood Rite? My Dilemma

Indeed, Ogwu-Uburu was close to Okpanku. It shares a common boundary with Amaeze Okpanku, my village. There was a famous market in Uburu called Nkwuru where my people went to buy salt since it is naturally abundant there. When water is fetched from the river there and boiled, it leaves salt residue, which is collected and used as table salt. This made Uburu a popular community at the time. Uburu people also came to Afor Okpanku market to sell their salt and to buy yams and other items they needed.

The road from Amaeze to Uburu was not passable by car. It was a winding road leading from bushes through forests and cutting through streams and the dangerous Ivo River. Therefore, though Uburu was close to Amaeze Okpanku, accessing it was difficult and perilous. Boats were required to cross the Ivo River during the rainy season, and at some point a rope bridge was built by the locals, using thick forest ropes and wood called *akwa eriri*.

At Uburu, I lived in Eze Nwabo's house. His son, Sunday Eze Nwabo, was already a student at St. Paul's Catholic School. Eze Nwabo, who agreed to accommodate me at his home, was a good friend of Okorie Ngwoke, who was from Amaeze and my father's friend. Eze Nwabo also agreed to accommodate my friend Sylvanus Ngwoke Okorie, son of Okorie Ngwoke. So, together with our parents, Sylvanus and I set out for Uburu. We carried our clothes, school items, and—most importantly—foodstuffs. At Uburu, Eze Nwabo handed Sylvanus and me over to his first wife, Umahi Ogo. He had little or no love for her, but we had no way of knowing this at the time.

· · · · · ·

The Teacher Boy

Before we arrived at their home, Eze Nwabo had already relocated to a farmhouse somewhere far away, with his second wife. There, he cultivated many hectares of farmland. They had made camp on this farm, and he rarely returned home to be with the first wife. Umahi Ogo fed us kindly only when we had foodstuffs in large supply. As soon as the food was no longer plentiful, she would say there was no more available and feed us whatever she thought was best. When our food was gone, we were on our own, staying hungry for days until our parents brought us more supplies. We were under immense hardship, as we were not allowed to cook our own meals.

Another colleague of ours, Mathias Uzoigwe, lived in a nearby compound and faced a similar challenge. We formed a strong friendship based on our shared hardship. We came up with a common way of greeting one another whenever we crossed paths. As soon as one of us set eyes on the other, the first words would be, "How many?"

And the response would be "Two" or maybe "Three."

This was how we communicated the number of boluses of fufu we swallowed before setting out for the day or to school.

Uburu's market was operational two days a week: the *Oge Ukwu* and *Oge Nta* market days. On *Oge Ukwu* market day, we did not go to school but to the Esu Riverbank to meet our parents, who arranged to bring food for us. If this food came, we were in heaven until it got exhausted. And when our food was exhausted, we survived by scavenging for food or eating fruits we found in the bushes. Once, we took some of Umahi Ogo's palm kernels to eat and were starved from afternoon until the following morning, with a serious warning not to take anything belonging to her, even if it was something as small and unimportant as a palm kernel.

In school at Uburu, we had a lovely time. We played and participated in various sports, including high jump, athletics, and football. Racing was my passion as I was already tall with long legs suitable for the sport.

On Saturdays and Sundays, we went into the forests to search for firewood and bring it back, so Umahi Ogo could heat salt water and get salt to sell at the market.

· · · · · ·

6. School or Ijiegbe *Manhood Rite?*

Soon came a big challenge that could have thwarted my father's ambition to see his son educated. It was 1951. I had finished Standard V at St. Paul's, Uburu, and needed to proceed to St. Anthony's Catholic School, Ishiagu, for Standard VI since my school in Uburu did not yet have the Standard VI class. This was also the year when the boys of my age-grade in Okpanku were to be initiated into manhood by passing and following the traditional *Ijiegbe* rites.

Ijiegbe, also called *Inwuegbe*, was so important a rite that if one failed to go through it with his mates in the year when it was their turn—say he missed the target of the egg set out for him to shoot at—he was regarded as a weakling. He would be made a caricature and not taken seriously in the community. It was a terrible misfortune not to partake in it when it was the year for one's age mates to perform the *Inwuegbe* or *Ijiegbe* or to fail to shoot down the egg target that admitted one into the process.

When our time for *Ijiegbe* came, my friends Hyacinth Okoro, Sylvanus Okorie, and Emmanuel Okorie dropped out of school and returned to Okpanku to perform the *Inwuegbe* rite. I was perplexed. It was the first of the many challenging dilemmas I would face in life. If I continued with my education and did not go for *Ijiegbe*, I would have no voice, I would also become unimportant in my community, and my family and I would become a laughingstock, even if I had all the education in the world.

What do I do? This question ate at me.

My father Okereke Abara's hunger for education was stoked by his experience in the native court at Ishiagu and his travels to faraway places for land adjudication. He knew—more than the fathers of my friends who dropped out to follow through with the *Ijiegbe* rites—that education was important and could foresee that it would be far more important than *Ijiegbe* in the future. He knew that if I continued with my education, I would be laughed at and insulted by my peers, but it would be nothing compared with the humiliation I would face in the future if I did not complete school. To prove it and make me believe him, he invited me to have a conversation with him.

I told my father that I would not be able to bear the shame that

· · · · · ·

The Teacher Boy

would befall me if I did not perform the *Ijiegbe* traditional manhood rites with my mates. It was difficult to put into words the shame that came with not performing the rites. It was common to daydream of the day, as it was akin to a day of graduation into adulthood for many young people at the time. It was what we talked about on the way to school and on our way back. It was what we talked about when we played and when we gathered to converse. We pictured ourselves, nude from the waist upwards and our bodies glistening with camwood mixed with water. Most importantly, we pictured ourselves with our Dane guns, trotting the village, gathering at the road junctions, the village square, and the market area to release shots into the air. There was no feeling greater than knowing that the most beautiful of the maidens in the village would admire your taut muscles as you lifted your gun to shoot into the air. I knew that most of the young girls admired us and wanted our company. I could not imagine not joining my colleagues.

In 1951, there were no educated persons in Okpanku as such, though we now have them by the hundreds. So, there was no one we could look up to or aspire to be like, like a professor or an engineer or a medical doctor. The idea of role models since the creation of the world has been to encourage people to look up to another who achieved success and distinguished himself, in modeling their own ambition and behavior. If there were people who went through education and became successful, it would have been easier for many to see the value of education. And the number of school dropouts at the time would have been reduced to the barest minimum. Most of the men who served as court clerks and interpreters and the like were not exactly educated. They were people trained by the European missionaries. So, one could argue that if they could rise to such positions of importance without education, then there was no need for it.

Those who dropped out could not see life beyond Okpanku. They did not understand or even know what went on in the outside world. Therefore, choosing between continuing with education and partaking in the *Ijiegbe* rite was not a major decision. Many who dropped out did not think twice before they did. In fact, many had

······

6. School or Ijiegbe *Manhood Rite?*

dropped out for things of less value than *Ijiegbe*, such as the distance between their villages and their schools.

Again, my father invited me to have a conversation with him, and we reached an agreement.

"You will do the *Ijiegbe*," he informed me, to my utmost happiness. "But not all of it."

I was astounded. *What did he mean by that?*

"You are aware that to be initiated into *Ijiegbe* rites, you have to shoot an egg and be sure that the gun does not fall out of your hands?"

"I am aware of that," I assured him.

"I have bought a gun for you," he said.

He proceeded to show me the gun. It was a long Dane gun, with the barrel polished and shiny. The butt made of wood was painted and looked like it was polished with a shoe polish. I gulped saliva. I could not wait to hold the gun in my hands. I imagined how my friends would feel seeing me run around the community with them, brandishing our guns. I imagined the look of love and envy in the eyes of the maidens when they saw me with it.

"Here is my proposal. The time for you to go to Ishiagu to register for Standard VI is now. If you do not go to Ishiagu but follow through with the process of *Ijiegbe*, you would miss school registration and will have to wait for another year. But there is no rule in Okpanku that says that one who has been initiated into the process of *Ijiegbe* must follow through with it until the end. There is no rule that says that you must have *odo* rubbed all over your body and run around the village shooting your gun in the air. Therefore, what will happen is that I have bought you a gun indicating my agreement for you to join your mates in participating in the *Ijiegbe* rite for this year." He handed the gun to me.

It felt heavy in my hands. I was delighted.

"I will summon our kinsmen. We will set the target for you. If you do it successfully and the gun does not fall out of your hands, then it will be announced that you are now part of your age-grade

· · · · · ·

that will perform *Ijiegbe* this year. After that, you will give me back the gun and leave for Ishiagu for your education." His gaze was on my face as he talked; he was watching and gauging my reactions.

He knew that he was treading a sensitive path. It was a topic that was dear to every young Okpanku boy. He needed to convince me to follow this path of education, which he chose for me. Of course, he did *Ijiegbe* during his own time and knew the importance. He knew that I was avoiding humiliation in the presence of my peers, to not be seen as a weakling.

"While other boys run around with *odo* rubbed on their bodies, shooting their guns into the air, you will be at St. Anthony's Catholic School, Ishiagu, studying to become the man they will never become. After the period of one month has elapsed, when it is time for Afor Aja Festival, the grand finale of the *Ijiegbe* rite, you will return from Ishiagu and collect your gun. You can then follow your mates to Afor and perform the final rites. That way, no one will say that you did not participate in the *Ijiegbe* rites. And you will have become a man."

I thought about his proposal. It made sense. Besides, if I went to St. Anthony's, Ishiagu, for Standard VI and completed it—even after my friends had dropped out to participate fully in the *Ijiegbe* rite—I would be the first from Amaeze to graduate from primary school with a Standard VI certificate. This enticed me more.

My father said, "But do you think that your friends who dropped out for *Ijiegbe* are better than you? Do you think that their fathers love them more than I love you? My decision for you to pursue the White man's knowledge is not because I want to go against our cultural values like *Ijiegbe* but because I know that it will distinguish you from your peers in the future. To prove to you that I love you, you are aware that I have found a wife for you, a girl from a very good family."

I nodded.

In 1949, my father found for me a wife, a girl who was nine years old then and a daughter of his good friend. All that was remaining was for me to finish my education.

And the next announcement swept me off my feet. "Most

・・・・・・

6. School or Ijiegbe *Manhood Rite?*

importantly, I am going to give you a chieftaincy title, one greater than *Ijiegbe*. I will perform the *Ima Inyinya* chieftaincy rite for you, which will make you a Mazi*. When people address you, after I have bought the horse for you and performed the title, they will address you as Mazi Uzoigwe Okereke. None of your friends will be addressed as that, at least not at your age."

I asked if he was serious. "Don't I need to be there to perform the horse title?"

"You do not need to be there. *Ima Inyinya* is greater than *Ijiegbe* because it is a title reserved only for the wealthy. It takes a lot of wealth to accomplish, but I will do it for you. That way, you will not be on the same level as your contemporaries. While you all would have become men after performing *Ijiegbe*, you will be greater in class than them all. You will be a Mazi. And with your education, you will be greater in knowledge than those World War II returnees."

This gladdened my heart the most.

* * *

As mentioned earlier, 1951 was a critical year in my life. It was the year that could have made or marred my life. It was the year I would have dropped out of school to perform the *Ijiegbe* rite, so I could be initiated into manhood, but my father's love for education saved me. He made me a deal I could not refuse. I became a man, successfully shooting the target set for me without my gun dropping out of my hands, and returned on Afor Aja to perform the final rites of the *Ijiegbe*. I also became a *Mazi*, as he bought the horse and performed the *Ima Inyinya* title for me.

Standard VI was the climax of my educational pursuit. I had come a long way: Infant I to Standard II at Okpanku; Standard III in Ndeaboh, 10 miles distant; and then Standards IV and V at St. Paul's Catholic School, Uburu, where life was also difficult. Now, it was time to move again. One of the things that made schooling difficult at the time was the constant relocation to faraway com-

---

*Mazi is a title reserved for only those that have performed the horse acquisition ceremony.

munities to board with families with whom one had no blood relationship.

My family had no relatives at Ishiagu, so there was that challenge of where I would live, yet again. A friend of mine who was a Standard V pupil of St. Anthony's Catholic School, Ishiagu, introduced me to Oshi Ajah, a gunpowder trader who often came to Okpanku to sell his gunpowder and its accessories. My father contacted Oshi Ajah. Since my father was a customer who patronized him as a hunter (and a good one at that) and who also used to give him meat and invite him to drinks, my father made a plea that he accommodate me in his home at Ishiagu. The trader agreed.

A day before the start of school, an Eke day, my parents and I set out for Ishiagu. We carried with us my bags, possessions, and school items. We carried with us foodstuffs, enough to last me a long time, including one fully roasted grasscutter. My mother also had such items as oil, pepper, salt, and ingredients for making soup; my father included yams. We arrived in Ishiagu, and because it was a market day, Oshi Ajah was busy. He accepted me and all the items we brought and promised my parents that he was going to take proper care of me. My parents bade me goodbye and left to return to Amaeze Okpanku.

The next day, Oshi Ajah's children took me to school, where I met most of my old classmates and friends from St. Paul's Catholic School, Uburu, and even from St. Paul's Catholic School, Okpanku. At Ishiagu, the system was different. I was in the senior class and studies were taken seriously. The teachers were more curious, better equipped, and more attentive to their duties. The headmaster was also hardworking and took his work seriously. The priest in charge of the parish, Father Coleman, taught Religious Knowledge every Wednesday. In this school, Mass on Sundays and benedictions were compulsory, and every pupil was expected to belong to a particular handwork group.

The school handwork teacher who taught us cane-chair making, Mr. Nwaozor, was harsh and strict. If one did not bring canes for the handwork, then he faced serious punishment. On some weekends, I trekked from Ishiagu to Amaeze Okpanku so I could go to a forest called Ofia Ibeku Amaeze where cane wood was in abundance

• • • • • •

6. School or Ijiegbe *Manhood Rite?*

to fetch some cane. It was also an opportunity for me to gather foodstuffs to take back to school. To carry cane and enough foodstuffs to last for a long time was difficult as the route was long—about 10.8 miles—and treacherous. Oshi Ajah's wife was also a difficult woman, though not as mean as the other women I lived with at Ndeaboh and Uburu. Whenever I did not return with food she considered sufficient to feed me during my stay at her home, she would become antagonistic and harsh.

Oshi Ajah also made me his sales boy. Every Eke and Afor market day, he took me to the market and gave me some carbide, gunpowder, and other accessories to sell. At the end of the market day, when we returned, he would summon me to give account of what I sold. I would present a summary of the money made from all the sales. But after my presentation, he would frown and berate me, saying that that was not how to take stock or present accounts as a trader. He always wanted me to account for them item by item. He wanted to know how much carbide, how much gunpowder, and how many of each other item I took to the market, what was sold, and what was left.

"Sylvester. This is not how to do trading, and this is not accounting. Account should be detailed: I sold this number of cups of carbide for so much, and that number of cups of gun powder for so much. I don't want you giving me a summary of your total sales." Then, he would punish me for not knowing how to give proper account of my sales and, most times, starve me of food. This training helped me years later when I started my own shop. It was also what helped me learn bookkeeping and prompted me to start a diary to keep the day-to-day accounts of my life.

At Oshi Ajah's home, I was inundated with so much domestic work that it became difficult to concentrate on my studies. I was either fetching firewood in the forest or water from the river or going to sell this or that for my master. Aside from these duties, it was not a difficult life, when compared to what I faced in Uburu and Ndeaboh. After my first term holiday at St. Anthony's, Ishiagu, I relocated to the village of Ngwogwo in Ishiagu, which was even farther away from Amaeze Okpanku.

· · · · · ·

The Teacher Boy

At Ngwogwo, I lived with a classmate named Donald Ajanne Uka. With him, my academics improved because I had more time for my studies. We were also inspired greatly by our class teacher, Mr. Eugene Anyata, a well-trained and motivated teacher. He handled all the subjects he taught us with perfection. Through him, our class performed so well and broke a record in St. Anthony's Catholic School, Ishiagu, such that all 36 of us scored 100 percent pass in our First School-Leaving Certificate examinations.

After Standard VI, I returned to Amaeze Okpanku from Ishiagu. My parents were happy. I was the first person in Amaeze to achieve this great feat of finishing Standard VI. When the results were released, my uncle, Joseph Abara, read them to my parents, who were jubilant. They threw a party in celebration, and I became the envy of my peers and colleagues. It did not take long to begin to see the wisdom in my dad's decision as my friends, especially Hyacinth Okoro, Emmanuel Okorie, and Mathias Uzoigwe, who dropped out of St. Paul's, Uburu, to perform the *Ijiegbe* rite, began preparing to return to Ishiagu to resume Standard VI.

7

The Teacher Boy

Okereke Abara, my father, was more than delighted that his son was the first graduate of Standard VI from Amaeze Okpanku. It became even more common to see him ordering the best palm wine to share with his friends. He also became more generous, giving out the game he caught from the bush to people. Sometimes, one would catch him smiling to himself and talking excitedly. It excited him that though his brothers and relatives dropped out of school, his own son stayed the course and finished, despite the challenge of relocating to different communities.

In 1952, something remarkable happened that instilled in me the virtues of generosity. This occurrence would teach me to be good to people and that the reward for generosity comes in ways that one might not imagine.

Mr. Edmund Akpa of the Mgbowo community, a respected headmaster, came to my father to buy yams. As my father was a renowned and respected yam farmer, many people came to him to buy sizable yams to eat or yam seedlings for cultivation. After he purchased the yams, my father, who had immense respect for educated people and teachers and believed that they were on the highest rung of the ladder of education, gifted the man some yams. This impressed the man immensely.

Meanwhile, the man had no money to pay for the yams he bought. He told my father that he would bring the money when he received his salary at month's end. My father agreed and told him to go with the yams and pay whenever he could. This surprised and impressed Mr. Akpa as well.

......

The Teacher Boy

The author preparing his lesson notes.

7. The Teacher Boy

A few days later, the headmaster came to collect the yams. He did not pick them up the other day because he had no means to carry them. That day, I was the one he met at home. He knew that I had completed Standard VI. He asked me if I would like to be a teacher, and I said that I would love to. He told me that there was an ongoing recruitment for auxiliary teachers and encouraged me to apply. Then, he wrote a draft application letter for me and advised that I use it as a model for mine, so it would stand out from the other applicants'. He also told me the day to take the letter to the Catholic parish at Awgu.

I went to St. Michael's Parish, Awgu, on January 1, 1952, as Mr. Akpa directed. There, I saw many other applicants from many communities. We met the Reverend Father McGreen and submitted our application letters. The reverend father was quite impressed by my application letter because it stood out from the others.

"Who is Sylvester Okereke?" the priest asked after a while. He was holding a letter in his hand.

I raised my hand and came out from the crowd, and he handed me a letter. It was an appointment letter, stating that I had been employed as an auxiliary teacher and posted to St. Paul's Catholic School, Okpanku.

There was no joy greater than that I would now be a teacher in a school in my community, in the same school where I studied as a child for four years, from Infant I to Standard II. I hurried home to share the news with my people. I was to begin work on March 3, 1952.

When I arrived home, I danced and sang and jubilated so much that people came out. My father and mother and siblings were in awe, asking what had happened to make me so jubilant.

"I have been employed as a teacher to work at St. Paul's!" I told them.

My father was jubilant. He began to dance. This was beyond his expectations. He knew that education was important and would make me a great man, but he did not know it was going to be so soon. A meal was prepared to celebrate me.

． ． ． ． ． ．

The Teacher Boy

Villagers came in to offer their congratulations.

"Have you seen that Okereke Abara's son who refused to join others to rub *odo* on his body and participate fully in *Ijiegbe* has now become a teacher?"

"He was the first to finish Standard VI and the first to become a teacher. Isn't that incredible?" they said to themselves.

Everyone was happy for me. Though I shot at the egg target to kick-start the process of *Ijiegbe* before returning to school and returned at the grand finale of Afor Aja to participate in *Ijiegbe* with my age mates, it was obvious that some villagers talked behind my back about how I chose to pursue education rather than partaking fully in the rites. But now they were surprised and jubilant. My father and I had been vindicated. The villagers soon began to tease my other age mates who dropped out to participate in *Ijiegbe*. They said those would now be at their homes eating food only. My mates who had dropped out for *Ijiegbe* realized then that they made the wrong choice. I was now the village hero—and the most eligible bachelor, had I not already had a girl betrothed to me.

By this time, St. Paul's Catholic School, Okpanku, had classes beyond Standard II. I returned to the school, discharging my duties conscientiously. I dressed for school like the most respected teacher in the world. And when I walked to the school and back, people paused to admire and praise me and talk about how my father's hard work and vision had been rewarded.

My first day at St. Paul's will remain in my memory until death. It was a remarkable one. I had a white-collar job; I could not believe it. Just few months before, I was a student, receiving punishments and going into the cane forests to harvest cane, but now I was a teacher.

That day, I arrived at school early, determined to utilize the opportunity to the best of my ability and to ensure that all the pupils under me got the best from me. I wanted not just to make my family proud but to be an exemplary teacher to the benefit of my community and the Catholic Church that gave me the opportunity to be useful. I went to the headmaster, Mr. Edmund Akpa, with my

• • • • • •

7. The Teacher Boy

appointment letter from St. Michael's Parish, Awgu. He was highly impressed.

After the morning assembly, he took me to the Infant II class and introduced me to the pupils. The class was divided into classes A and B. Before my arrival, another teacher, Mr. Patrick Orjiakor from Ndeaboh, had been handling both classes.

A note was circulated by the headmaster for a teachers' conference during the break period, and at the meeting he introduced me to the teachers and told them about me. I was then assigned to handle Infant II, Class B, and handed me a set of teaching materials, which included textbooks, an exercise book to serve as lesson notes, a class register, and a class diary.

I had a lively class with obedient and hardworking pupils. And soon, every pupil wanted to be in my class, for I was known for my physical education exercises and ability to use storytelling in teaching my students.

While in the school, I was grateful to have the support of other teachers who guided and trained me, especially Mr. Patrick Orjiakor and Mr. Fidelis Kama from Mgbowo. I was optimistic and hopeful that I would become a teacher to be reckoned with. And my parents were happy, especially when I received my first paycheck of £1. I recall how I felt the moment my headmaster handed me my paycheck. I could have sprouted wings and flown. I could become anything I wanted to be. That is what education does; it not only provides one with the means of livelihood but bolsters one's conviction that everything is possible.

That day, when I got home, I took the money to my father. He happily accepted it to look at it. Then, he instructed me to give it to my mother for safekeeping, which I did.

I remained in St. Paul's Catholic School until January 1, 1953, when I was posted to St. Joseph's Catholic School, Mpu. There, I worked with Mr. Bernard Abochi, a man from Nenwe, who was the headmaster, and two other staff. From there, I was deployed to St. Joseph's Extension School, Amachalla Mpu.

In those days, Mpu comprised such villages as Amachalla, Uke,

······

The Teacher Boy

Ubeagu, and Ovum. The councilors of these villages were charged with collecting ALC from every taxable adult in their villages to enable payment to the auxiliary teachers. While there at Mpu, I adopted a young boy named Damian Okoro as my godson. He lived with me and helped as my domestic staff or "houseboy." The school system had a policy that grown-up boys were to sleep in their teachers' quarters at night since the quarters were on the school premises. That way, they helped provide security, and the teachers also ensured that they studied their books and did their homework. Some of the boys who regularly spent the night at the teachers' quarters were Felix Oshi, Edwin Anyim, Benjamin Anya, and Ferdinand Ofili.

I worked at St. Joseph's Catholic School, Mpu, from January 1953 to December 31, 1955, teaching the Infant I and II classes.

* * *

It was when I started teaching that I began to see the importance of education. My father had been right all along; he knew that education accorded one with not just knowledge but respect and dignity. I was known as the first Amaeze man to finish Standard VI and the first to get a white-collar job and become a teacher, but I did not want to be the only one. I wanted more and more people to become like me and possibly greater than me.

So I began to petition the Reverend Father McGreen for an extension of St. Paul's Catholic School to Amaeze, so that children who could not attend school because it was too far away would have the opportunity to enroll. I offered to travel to Awgu to meet the reverend priest and plead with him to approve this extension.

In 1954, the Reverend McGreen consented, and approval was given for this extension. By then, I was at St. Joseph's, Mpu. To accommodate the school, I donated my family land for it. It was a vast area of land that could have been utilized for farming, but to the chagrin of my family and to the admiration of many, I donated this land to Amaeze for the school extension. A few other donors came forward as well and donated their lands in solidarity and support, and a mud house building of two classrooms was constructed by the

7. The Teacher Boy

people of Amaeze. The villages mobilized to make the mud blocks and provided the labor themselves, and, soon after, the building was ready. The Catholic Church mission provided zinc sheets and a carpenter to do the roofing.

I completed my assignment at St. Joseph's Catholic School, Mpu, in December 1955, and on January 1, 1956, I was transferred to the new school I pioneered, St. Paul's Catholic School, Amaeze Extension, to serve as its first teacher. I earlier contacted the parish priest, the Reverend McGreen, asking for him to approve a name for the school, but he asked me to name the school with his approval. I named the school St. Theresa's School, Amaeze, in memory and recognition of Mrs. Theresa Ivoke, the pioneer Christian woman from Amaeze. I remained in the new school until December 31, 1956.

The author's son, Professor Chukwumerije Okereke, visiting Community Primary School Amaeze, formerly St. Theresa's School, Amaeze, where he attended primary school (this is the same school that the author founded).

• • • • • •

The Teacher Boy

On January 1, 1957, I was transferred to St. Mary's Catholic School in the community of Ihe, where I taught until December 1957. The transfers to different communities always reminded me of moving from Okpanku to Ndeaboh, to Uburu, and to Ishiagu in search of education. The only difference was that now I was my own man, and I had my monthly salary and the respect of the people. The headmaster of the school at Ihe was Mr. Godwin U. Ochi of Ogugu, who once taught at St. Paul's Catholic School, Okpanku, when the school was at Oji and I was a pupil. Back then, he was an auxiliary teacher. St. Mary's Catholic School, Ihe, was one of the biggest schools then with so many teachers—about 12 of them on staff. I took my younger brother Louis to this school and enrolled him there and cared for him as well, providing all he needed to go to school.

I became friends with most of the teachers since by this time a few other Okpanku boys had become teachers as well. On our way to our different schools, we rode our bicycles. I rode my Raleigh bicycle to Ihe, Patrick C. Okorie rode to Agbudu, Francis O. Agwu rode to Agbogugu, and Edwin Aroh rode to Ituku. On weekends, we met up and rode back to Okpanku with our heads held high, for it was common for teachers to have bicycles. They were among the few, except wealthy yam farmers, who could afford it. Others watched us in admiration, and this spurred many to enroll their children in school.

It was at this time that it was agreed that I could start courting my betrothed, Virginia Orieji, the daughter of Onu Makwe, officially. By this time, she was enrolled to start learning hand sewing in preparation for our marriage, which happened that year in 1957.

8

And Death Broke Me into Pieces

It was Queen Elizabeth II who once said that grief is the price we pay for love. I did not know and could never imagine that I would pay this price so early in my life. But then, as saddening as this statement from the Queen makes me feel, one realizes upon some serious thought that it is true. For when a loved one passes, we are thrown into a state of confusion and despair. This combination of confusion and despair, for me, was grief.

In 1949 when I was in Standard IV, my father—as his way of proving his love for me and appreciation for respecting his wishes to pursue the White man's knowledge—found a wife for me. It was not something I was thinking about or could have imagined. I was just 12 years old at the time, not that there were not other boys my age whose families had found them wives-to-be. It was common for wealthy parents to betroth the daughters of their friends to their sons. Then, they would watch the girl grow and ripen into a young woman, while occasionally bringing her gifts and presents and ensuring that she received the best of care and love. Sometimes, the girl could come stay in the family of her betrothed and be taken care of until they were both considered mature enough for marriage. At this time, there was nothing like premarital sex, and young people did not think about it. When a betrothed boy and girl ran into each other on a pathway or at school or at the village market, the most they could do was smile at each other and go their separate ways.

At the time, I did not expect that I would be given a wife. My father was too much invested in my education to care about anything

. . . .

The Teacher Boy

else—or so I thought. But that was not to be the case. Come to think of it, my father was the only son of his father through his mother Ukpai Njoku, though his father had sons from his other wives. He must have felt he needed to have his son marry early so that he could begin to try for sons. Male children were valued immensely at the time in Igboland. My father's own father was also the only son of his father through his mother, Orieji Abara Onu. So, whichever way one thought about it or argued it, that might have been the case. But that day in 1951 when we had the conversation about not abandoning schooling to go for the *Ijiegbe* rite, he did mention that to prove his love for me, he would give me the *Mazi* title reserved solely for one who had taken the horse title and that he had found a wife for me.

I recall the day my father began the process of my betrothal in 1949, while I was home for vacation after the third term of my Standard IV. Virginia was just nine years old at the time. That day, my father and his close friend, Onu Makwe, were sitting by my father's yam barn, drinking and enjoying the keg of freshly tapped palm wine he bought that day and washing their wine down with well-prepared bushmeat.

Then, he summoned me. When I came and stood in their presence, he said to me, "*Nna ogo m.*" This was the affectionate name he called me, having named me after my mother's father. "There is a gift I want to present to you," he said.

At the mention of a gift, I was elated and surprised as well, and I waited eagerly to learn what this gift was.

He said, "I have found a wife for you, a girl named Virginia Orieji, the daughter of my friend here." He nodded in the direction of his friend, whose gaze was focused on me, watching my every reaction, a joyous smile on his face. "I want her to be your wife. As you are aware, she is a beautiful girl from a respected home." Thinking that I might object, he said, "I do not want you to give me a response now. No, that is not what I am saying." He took a sip from his gourd cup of palm wine and, while smiling, said, "Go there in the evening and see her. Then, come back and tell me what you think of her, if

・・・・・・

8. And Death Broke Me into Pieces

there is anything. Tell me if you like her enough to be your wife. All right?"

Most times, when parents found a partner for their children, they sought no input. They simply told you who was found for you, you followed the process, and the person became your wife or husband. But my father, whose love for me made him respect me as well, especially because I was following his vision for education and was doing well in school, gave me an option. He asked me to go see the girl in the evening and report whether I liked her. I thanked him and his friend and left their presence.

That day, my head was in confusion. It felt like people were whispering different thoughts in my ears and messing with my head. On one hand, I was excited; on the other, I was confused. I did not know what it entailed for her to be my wife. I did not know what I was expected to do or how I was to go about it. But I did not wait for evening to come, as he instructed. I hurried off to Onu Makwe's home and saw Orieji. Of course, it was not the first time I had seen her. Before, I used to see her as the daughter of my father's friend and a girl from my village, but now I had to start seeing her as my potential wife. She was a beautiful girl, no doubt. She had white, calm eyes; a kind smile; and a face that showed curiosity. I hurried back home.

When I got home, my heart pounded in excitement that was a mix of worry and expectation. So, I went to my mother for guidance and counsel. I told her what my father had said and that I had already gone to see the girl.

"Oh, you have gone to see her already?"

"Yes, I have," I informed her. "But Mama, I do not know anything about marriage. I do not know how to go about it. What should I tell Papa?"

My mother smiled at me and said, "Did your father ask that you do anything, like bring money for the marriage process?"

I shook my head. "No, he did not."

"Did he ask that you take care of the girl or her family?"

"No," I said. "He did not say that. He only asked that I go see the girl and give him a response."

・・・・・・

The Teacher Boy

"Then, go tell him that you have seen the girl and that you are in agreement."

Obviously, this matter had been discussed with my mother. It is possible that it was she who suggested Orieji, Onu Makwe's daughter. Onu Makwe was the man who always followed my father to Ishiagu for the court hearings. He was also the one who accompanied my father on all his land adjudication trips to Akaeze and faraway Abakaliki. So, they had come a long way. The marriage between myself and Onu Makwe's daughter was a way to cement the long-lasting relationship between our families. It was the norm at the time, and it was expected that if we got married, the friendship would continue beyond our parents.

That evening, I went to my father. This time, he was no longer with his friend. I told him that I went to Onu Makwe's house and that I saw the girl. "I have done as you said," I told him. "I have seen the girl. I agree with your proposal."

After that day, whatever happened between my family and the girl's family was not my concern or business. My parents began to take care of the girl and her family all by themselves. They sent them foodstuffs after harvests; they sent the girl and her mother gifts during festivals like *Omoha* or *Aja* or *Iboafo*. All that was required of me was that I mind my business and concentrate on my studies. This kind of betrothal lasted for many years, until the betrothed was matured and ready. Therefore, it was capital intensive, and only the wealthy embarked on it. It was rare for proletariats to betroth a girl to their son.

This betrothal did not exactly register in my mind so much, as my parents were the ones who took care of everything, until I got a job as a teacher. In addition to the care and love my family showed Onu Makwe's family and Virginia especially, they advised that I start sending her gifts after I completed Standard VI and started working as a teacher.

So, every month when I received my salary, I took out a little money to buy Virginia such presents as pomade and soap and beads. She was aware, of course, of our betrothal. So, whenever we ran into

· · · · · ·

8. And Death Broke Me into Pieces

each other on the road, we stopped to greet each other. It was usually a brief encounter as we were both shy, though I always tried to mask my shyness.

By the end of 1956 up to early 1957, when I was 20, it was decided by both families that it was time for us to be married. We, therefore, formally began courting, and I decided to register her to learn a skill since she did not go to school, and on January 3, 1957, an agreement to train her in hand sewing was signed. My father paid for the registration.

She was apprenticed under Mrs. Alice Achi, the wife of the headmaster of St. Paul's Catholic School, Okpanku, at the time. She was to also receive marriage counseling from her.

On December 28, 1957, Virginia and I were joined in holy matrimony at St. Michael's Catholic Church, Awgu, with Mr. and Mrs. Mark Chukwurah as sponsors/witnesses.

Barely 15 days later, Virginia fell ill. Her health deteriorated so badly that my world came crashing down in the series of events that followed. On January 12, 1958, she was admitted at the University of Nigeria Teaching Hospital, Enugu. She was there until January 20, when she was discharged and referred to Joint Hospital, Awgu, for checkups. On our way back to Okpanku, she relapsed, and we headed straight to Joint Hospital, Awgu, where she was readmitted on February 3, 1958. On March 28, 1958, she passed on.

The death of my young wife, Orieji Virginia Onu Makwe, left me confused. It made my heart sink so low into the vast ocean in my heart that it nearly consumed me. First, I was a young man, and I had just lost my wife. I had just lost a wife I was married to for just three months and a friend I had known since I was a child and whom I was betrothed to for nine years.

I had known this girl all my life. Then, we were betrothed for nine years, seeing each other every time I was home from school when I became a teacher in 1952 until when I married her in late 1957. Before marriage, I bought her gifts and already saw her as my wife. Her death, just shortly after our marriage, was shocking to me.

• • • • • •

The Teacher Boy

It shattered my young heart that just a few months after I became a married man, I was a widower. It was the hardest shock of my life.

There was little or no honeymoon. We were yet to do the traditional *ibu-ulo*, which would see her parents present us with her dowry, consisting of household items and assorted gifts. I had only paid her bride price and done the other traditional rites such as *Inye Ive-l'eka*, *ikpolulu*, and *ibu-anu*, and taken her to the altar. I could not comprehend it. Try as I might, it was difficult to put the shock into words.

In Okpanku, during my childhood, as I mentioned earlier, marriages everywhere took place during *Afor Ajah* Festival. Everyone who was to get married began the process; in the months and weeks leading up to the festival and on *Afor Ajah* day, just as the boys were being admitted into manhood through the *Ijiegbe* rite and were shooting their Dane guns at Afor market, the girls in the fattening room would leave for their husbands' homes. But by 1957, when we got married, there had been a significant shift and change in this practice due to the influence of Christianity, and people could choose when to hold their marriage ceremonies. This explains why I took my wife to the altar in December. By 1957, Christianity had spread, and the church had grown. Many people had embraced education and Christianity, and not everyone participated in *Ijiegbe*. Fewer families allowed their girls to go through the process of circumcision and the fattening room.

Though the tradition of marriage on Afor Ajah day had changed, many others remained. One of these was the tradition in Okpanku that a man was not to go close to his wife's corpse and a woman was not to go close to her husband's corpse, until burial. This tradition is still in practice today, but, in my case, I was with Virginia when she passed. Perhaps the ancestors and elders of Okpanku had not considered the possibility that a man could be with his wife in the hospital, caring for her, and she would pass on or that one of them would pass while traveling with the other in a vehicle.

When Virginia passed in my hands in the hospital, I was devastated. What was I to do? I was probably the first man in Okpanku to

• • • • • •

8. And Death Broke Me into Pieces

be close and alone with the corpse of his wife at that time. The hospital insisted I clean and dress her up and take her to the mortuary, and the nurses refused to assist. After I cleaned her up and dressed her, I went to the security in the hospital and pleaded that they help me carry her to the mortuary. They also refused.

"Carrying corpses is not part of the job we are recruited to do here," they said.

There was nothing I could do. I lifted Virginia's body all by myself, carried her outside, and began to head to the mortuary. It was not a long distance, but it seemed like forever. Of course, she was heavy just as my heart was. No one in my family, not even in Okpanku, knew that she had died; there was no means of communication then as we now have with phones. How was I to break the news to her family that their daughter whom I had married a few months earlier had passed on? At some point, I dropped Virginia's body on the ground and paused to rest my aching feet and arms. When I finally got to the mortuary, the attendants also refused to help me take her inside and or help place her on the platform meant for corpses. They responded just as the security people had, explaining that it was not part of their job description. I had to wait to gain enough strength and courage before carrying her inside and heaving her onto the pavement erected for that purpose. By this time, my tears had soaked my shirt.

Before then, in fact, since I was born, I had never sniffed tobacco snuff, but after I deposited my wife's body, I saw one of the morgue security men bring out his tobacco snuff container and, using his index finger, scoop a heap into his cupped hand. I asked him to share his tobacco snuff with me, and he agreed. From that day on, I began to take tobacco and did not stop until years later, when I was about to go for further studies.

I did not sleep that night, as she passed in the evening and I did all that work of carrying her body to the morgue. I could not sleep. I joined the night watchmen to keep watch. Before she passed, I went to the parish house at Holy Rosary Catholic Church, Awgu, a short distance away from the hospital, to bring the priest to give her the sacrament of Extreme Unction, now called Anointing of the Sick, fearing she was about to pass. It was after she received the sacrament from the priest and I escorted the priest back to the parish house and returned—just short of two hours after she received the sacrament—that she passed. I hurried back to the parish house to inform the priest that my wife had passed.

He asked that I inform an ambulance driver who worked for the church, so that the next day he would convey me and the body home to Okpanku.

The next morning, I went to the ambulance driver, and we went back to the morgue. But that morning, on my way to the church to call the ambulance driver, I got to a bridge and stopped. I was sobbing. My head was throbbing. I was confused and did not know what to do. How was I going to explain that Virginia had passed to my family and her family? I decided then that it would be best if I killed myself. I made up my mind to lie down on the bridge and wait until a vehicle came and crushed me. So, I did just that. Not long after, a bus approached with great speed, not knowing that someone was stretched out at the center of the bridge. The driver was surprised when I did not leave the road. He engaged his brakes and was lucky not to hit me, for his vehicle stopped not far from me. He was aghast.

He alighted from his vehicle in fury, cussing. *"Ekwensu!* Satan! You are looking for who to put in trouble!"

Then, he grabbed me and threw me across the bridge into the bush. The river was dry as it was March and the dry season. So, I fell on the hard, sun-dried earth and sustained bruises on my knees and ankles and elbow. I was there for a moment, crying, hopeless and helpless. It was then I realized the truth in C.S. Lewis's statement: "No one ever told me that grief felt so much like fear."

The ambulance driver and I drove back to the hospital and to the morgue. He said that he was not going to help me carry the body into his ambulance because it was not his job. The body had swollen by then and was beginning to give off a faint odor. The driver and the mortuary attendants watched as, again, I lifted the body and carried it into the ambulance. It was a herculean task, much more

8. And Death Broke Me into Pieces

difficult this time. We began to head to Okpanku. It was a journey of 20 miles.

There was no means of communicating to my people what had happened. It was 1958, and the only means of communication was sending people to deliver messages or through letter writing. Neither option was available to me at the time.

The ambulance soon got to *Ivo Agbalaka* bridge, which was made of wood and ropes and sticks and which no bus could cross. So, the driver terminated his journey and ordered that I offload the corpse from his vehicle. I did. I lifted the corpse again and placed it by the side of the bridge. Then, I used one of my late wife's gowns to cover her body, from head to toe, before speedily riding to the next Okpanku village, called Okpu, with my bicycle, which I had also carried alongside the corpse in the ambulance.

At Okpu, I found a man named Chukwu Anyim and told him what had happened. He came with me to the bridge and agreed to stand guard over the corpse while I rode back to Amaeze to a distance of about 7 km to inform my people.

Just as I entered Amaeze, I bumped into my father. He was headed to Awgu to visit me at the hospital and was shocked to see me. I broke down as I told him what happened and where the corpse was. My father was devastated and scared, for I was an Okpanku man and had been in close contact with my wife's corpse. It had never happened before. We went back home and alerted some men of the Umuogwudu family, and a few young boys were selected to go to Ivo Bridge on bicycles to bring home Orieji's corpse for burial. More villagers were informed, and Christians and the priest gathered and prayed for her before she was laid to rest.

After the burial, I was given a week off duty by my headmaster, Mr. G.U. Achi. I had become sick after all the episodes of taking care of Virginia while she was sick and bringing the corpse back to Okpanku.

It worried my father that I was going to die. This worried him so much for he was a man who believed in the tradition and practices of the Okpanku people and did all within his power to keep to every

・・・・・・

one of them. But I assured him that nothing would happen to me. By then, my faith had been strengthened. I was made a catechist on January 25, 1958, just shortly before Virginia's passing, and was a devout Roman Catholic. I told him that I would tell the priest at St. Paul's Catholic Church of my encounter with my wife's corpse and ask him to pray for me. I assured my father that nothing would happen to me.

Soon after, I went to my priest and told him everything. He assured me that nothing was going to happen to me and prayed for me. Later that same year, I was made a divisional councilor.

* * *

The death of my wife was not going to be the only thing that would hit me hard. Five years later, in December 1963, my dear father passed. He fell sick and was taken to a hospital at Afikpo. After a while, he was discharged, but his health continued to deteriorate. Just after he was discharged, he instructed me on how to harvest his yams. I got laborers to work with me, and we harvested his yams.

One day, he summoned and thanked me for being a loyal son, for agreeing to pursue the White man's education, and for taking care of the family since I began working as a teacher. He encouraged me to continue to take care of the family, especially my siblings.

My father asked to be baptized so he could become a Christian. I readily agreed and sent for Mr. Francis Awgu. Even though I was a catechist, I felt my father would not appreciate it if I did it myself. It is said that a prophet is not recognized and respected in his hometown, after all. Francis Awgu was the first catechist of Okpanku before me and the second teacher after me. So, on December 17, 1963, my father received the sacrament of baptism and was named Peter. Two days later, he passed on to the great beyond.

The day he passed was a dark one for me and for our family. It was a dark year. He was buried on December 20, 1963, following Okpanku traditional rites by traditional religious adherents, for he was a great and respected man.

Though my father was baptized before his death, I reasoned that he was a traditionalist all his life and would prefer that those

8. And Death Broke Me into Pieces

he associated with bury him with the full rites accorded to a chief. He was a *Mazi*, having taken the *Ima Inyinya* title. He was also an *Ogbuefi*, having taken the Igbo cow title and was the popular *Agulawu*, the leader of Etaovi-Okpanku Hunters Association.

． ． ． ． ． ．

9

A Politician at 21

It was Plato who once wrote that one of the penalties for refusing to participate in politics is that you end up being governed by your inferiors. Plato was right. I had always known this, even as a young man growing up in Okpanku.

At that time, there were few educated people. The warrant chiefs were handpicked by the British colonialists, who foisted those they believed to be loyal to them on the people. But I always believed that a time would come in my life when I would need to serve my people. Having been a teacher for six years and seen firsthand how the educated school administrators and the priests ran the schools and the church, I knew that the best that could happen to our communities was to have educated people in positions of leadership. If Paramount Chief Aja Ngwute and my father, Okereke Abara, who both had no education, could have strong vision for knowledge, enough to bring education to our people and make me go to school, I believed educated people could do better. They could achieve unimaginable feats. But what I did not know, at the time, was that I was going to be thrown into a leadership position at a very young age.

Becoming a teacher was indeed a great feat. People looked up to me, and my contemporaries admired and held me in awe and esteem. It was a life I prepared for, having gone through school and become a graduate of Standard VI, which was a mighty achievement for a boy from the hinterlands of Amaeze, Okpanku. But I did not prepare for political positions the way I prepared for an academic position. Although perhaps while I was preparing myself through school for teaching, I was also preparing for other positions in life. That could

......

9. A Politician at 21

be the truth. It could be that while one is equipping oneself with knowledge in a particular field, one does not know how that knowledge could be applied in other fields.

My venture into leadership began on September 28, 1958, when I was a young 21-year-old teacher. There was going to be a divisional council election to elect councilors who would represent the divisional wards under Awgu County Council. Before 1958, Okpanku had just one council ward, and it shared this ward with the community of Mpu.

Okpanku/Mpu Ward used to be represented at the Awgu County Council by Mr. Jeremiah Obasi, a position he had held since 1947. But after the Nigerian national population census of 1952–1953, Okpanku was split into two council wards, namely Okpanku I comprising the villages of Amabiriba, Amaogudu, Amagu, and Okpu, and Okpanku II comprising Amaeze, Ihuibe, and Uhuezeoke. And now Mpu had its own council ward. This new split, which created two council wards for my community, implied that Okpanku needed to elect two councilors, one for each of Okpanku I and II.

One day, while I was teaching in a classroom at St. Paul's Catholic School, a meeting was being held under a neem tree on the school premises. The leaders of Okpanku and officers from Awgu Divisional Council were deliberating on filling the two council ward positions. There was going to be an election, if need be, but I did not know what was being discussed for it was of no interest to me; after all, I was a young teacher.

Shortly afterwards, the local village councilor in charge of my village, a man named Ogwo Njoku, came into my class. He asked to speak with me and, when I stepped out of the class, he told me that he was asked by the community to inform me, as my village local councilor, that a decision was reached that there would be no election for the council wards because I had been chosen by the community as the one to represent Okpanku II as divisional councilor. This took my breath away. What would I do? I was just a boy.

He took me to the leaders of the community who were still gathered under the neem tree. Indeed, they had reached the decision that

· · · · · ·

The Teacher Boy

I would be their councilor. Jeremiah Obasi was to continue as councilor and represent Okpanku I. My father was not at that meeting; if he had been, I would have thought that he, being an immensely respected community leader, had influenced the decision. I told them that I needed to consult my family, and they agreed. One of the electoral officers from Awgu County Council asked if I was a registered voter. I told him I was registered. He told me to bring my credentials when I came back if I made up my mind to take up the offered position. I rode home as fast as I could to consult with my father.

It was the sort of bicycle journey on which the bicyclist might fall off. My heart beat loudly. I was confused. What was I going to say? How was I going to lead a whole community and represent them at a divisional council when there were other more qualified people from other communities? My heart was pounding heavily, and my feet shook on the pedals. I got home and told my father what had transpired.

"What do I do?" I asked him.

"You do not own yourself, my son," my father said. "I might have paid for your education, but our people say that the child belongs to the people, not to his parents only, or even to his family." Again, he said, "You do not own yourself. You are owned by the community. If Okpanku has asked that you serve them, then you will have to serve them."

I thanked him, took my credentials, and rode back to school.

When I got back to school, I went to my headmaster. I told him that I was offered a position to serve the people as a councilor and that I had told my father. He also advised that I accept the position. Then, I went to the leaders and elders of Okpanku gathered there at the neem tree and informed them that I agreed to serve as councilor. I also gave my voter's card and credentials to the electoral officers, and, by 4:00 p.m. that day, I was a divisional councilor.

Jeremiah Obasi and I went together to give the villagers an assortment of wines, shared across the villages of Okpanku, to thank them for putting their trust in us. To my colleagues, I also gave wines of all types and packets of biscuits for merriment, to share my joy

· · · · · ·

9. A Politician at 21

with them. While we made merry, some of the teachers said that I had become a beacon of hope and light for my people. Then, Patrick Ojiakor of Ndeaboh called me "Sy de Moon." And from then on, my nickname became "Sylvester the Moon" or "Sy de Moon," meaning "Sylvester, the moon (light) of his people."

That year, 1958, was already a big year for me, as I was also appointed the catechist of St. Paul's Catholic Church in January by the Reverend Father McGreen. Two months after, in March, I lost my wife. And in September I became a politician, a divisional councilor. Back then, serving in the divisional council was a part-time job, unlike in these modern times when politicians take the role as a permanent, fully paid job. We only went to the council on meeting days, while still holding our regular jobs.

Though I was a councilor, one could have ordinarily dismissed me; I was just a boy, after all, with no experience in politics. This worried me. Since I was chosen and given the opportunity to serve my people, I believed I needed to discharge my duties well. I also needed to ensure that I did not let them down. So, I came up with a political strategy that I suspect will impress even today's "political Maradonas."

I reasoned that since I did not know much about the customs and traditions of Okpanku or about diplomacy and adjudication, I needed the counsel and guidance of wise men from villages in my community. I thought long and hard about such men, and when I had their names, I approached them and told them that though I was their divisional councilor, I valued their wisdom and knowledge and wanted their guidance. They were very pleased by my request and readily agreed to mentor and guide me. So, if there was a dispute or deliberation to be had or a decision to be made about the people, I would first meet with these men selected from villages under my ward. Then, we would deliberate on the matter and come up with a decision, guided by the best moral, cultural, and traditional practices. And after such deliberations, I spoke with authority at the ward or community meeting. This gained me fame and respect from the community.

At the meeting, if anyone tried to oppose me or shut me up, believing I was a boy, the men would stand up to such people in my

· · · · · ·

The Teacher Boy

defense. Since they were respected men and people saw that they had my back, I gained more respect and honor. The men who agreed to work with me as guardians were my uncles Mazi Okereke Onu and Chief Ogbu Chukwu Itata, and my father Okereke Abara.

If there was a cultural dispute between the people of Amaeze, Amagu, and Uhuezeoke, then I would first approach these statesmen separately for advice and cultural clarification. And if there existed a discrepancy in their analyses, then I would invite them for a conversation over a keg of palm wine or two for reconciliation.

Having seen that tapping the rich knowledge of these men was beneficial to my ward and the community at large, I knew that I needed to be directly in touch with my constituents as their councilor, so that I would know their problems and needs and be able to report them to Awgu County Council. Thus, I invented the very first formal *Umunna* Association, consisting of members of the same *ikwu** of the Umuogwudu family. The meeting triggered the formation of other *Umunna* meetings. These *ikwu* meetings, which are still held today, have evolved into a strong force for dispute settlement and for helping needy members of the community. To this day it remains highly unusual for anyone to head to the police or to the court for adjudication without first reporting the matter to his *ikwu* for traditional adjudication.

It was not enough just to be selected. I also needed to fight my way into the leadership of the council by getting onto a good committee. So, I fought my way through strong bureaucracy, and after an election that was conducted among the 52 councilors who made up the council, I became vice chairman of the Roads and Works Committee of Awgu County Council. I served in this capacity from 1958 to 1962, when my tenure ended.

Elections were conducted by the district officer, the secretary of the council, the minutes clerk, and police officers. The election was by ballot. The councilor with the most votes cast for each committee headed the committee, while his running mate became the vice chairman of that committee.

---

*Kindred.

9. A Politician at 21

The following councilors emerged for various positions:

1. Chief G.U. Ochi—Chairman of Council
   Mr. A.O. Ude—Vice Chairman of Council
2. Hon. E. Iloka—Chairman of Finance, Staff and General Purposes Committee
   Mr. Emmanuel Umezuruike—Vice Chairman
3. Mr. Cosmas Eze—Chairman of Roads and Works Committee
   Mr. Sylvester Uzoigwe Okereke—Vice Chairman
4. Mr. F.O. Onyiba—Chairman of Public Health, Education, and Scholarship Committee
   Mr. Duke Mba—Vice Chairman

I cannot put into words how I felt about having such men as colleagues. Chief G.U. Ochi, who was the chairman of the council, was one of the pioneer teachers at St. Paul's Catholic School, Okpanku. I felt honored to be working, brainstorming, and sharing notes and ideas with such men.

As divisional councilor, I attended the general council meetings once a month, always on the last Saturday. Only the chairman of a committee was required to attend meetings twice per month, the general council on the last Saturday and committee meetings on the second Saturday.

The distance between Okpanku and Awgu is 20 miles, and the only way to reach the council headquarters was by trekking or riding on one's bicycle. On April 11, 1959, I bought a brand new Raleigh bicycle, which was a great feat to achieve back then. In fact, I was the third person in Amaeze and the first among my age-grade to own a Raleigh bicycle. The bicycle had a satchel on the back, on which I inscribed "I Shall Return by Sy. De Moon." This phrase was a reminder to myself to work hard and recover from the loss of my wife the year before.

To attend the council meeting, Jeremiah Obasi and I left by seven o'clock in the morning and rode to Afor Ndeaboh. There, we stopped at a local restaurant, had breakfast, and rested for a while

· · · · · ·

The Teacher Boy

before resuming our journey to the council headquarters at Awgu for our ten o'clock meeting.

Back then, the chairman of the council had veto power over all decisions. Though there were other councilors, he relied mostly on the chairmen of the committees, just as is done today. In modern times, chairmen of local government councils have so much uncontrolled power. Back then, there were more checks, but the chairman of a council and the chairmen of committees were honest and steadfast. Money budgeted for a program was spent on what it was meant for, unlike today when there is rampant embezzlement and mismanagement of funds.

Before my time in politics and before we began to have divisional heads, the political structure was such that the people were ruled by warrant chiefs who oversaw villages and communities. These warrant chiefs settled disputes and land cases and collected taxes, which they remitted to the colonial administration. The warrant chiefs had powers to avert police arrest and to also hand over an erring member of their village to the police. But the police could not make any arrests in the villages under their jurisdiction without first consulting with them.

The warrant chiefs derived their powers by the warrants of authority issued to them by the British colonial government. This started around 1890 and was further reinforced in 1900 by the Native Courts Proclamation* and a follow-up proclamation in 1901.† The 1900 proclamation created two categories of courts: the Minor Courts, comprising all courts presided over by a "native authority," and the "Native Councils," which were superior to the former. These Native Councils were presided over by British political officers and some Nigerian warrant chiefs. The political officers in the Native Councils also oversaw judicial proceedings and reported to district commissioners, who were members of the Supreme Court. Accordingly, a British political officer supervised all courts in his district

---

*Law No. 5.
†Law No. 25 of Southern Nigeria.

9. A Politician at 21

and sent appeals to district commissioners serving on the Supreme Court at the time.

Warrant chiefs served as members of the native courts. Obi Nwaonye of Okpu, Uzoigwe Uneke of Amaogudu, and Aja Elewe of Amaeze served as members of Ndeaboh Native Court, which administered all areas around my community back then. This system remained in place until the appointment of warrant chiefs was dropped, following the 1929 Women's Riots, when women across Eastern Nigeria protested the high-handedness of the warrant chiefs, especially high taxation. By 1930, warrant chiefs were removed from their positions of power, although some of them remained locally influential and even regained chieftaincy positions. Some of their descendants also inherited this influence and chieftaincy authority and are still wealthy today.

After the Women's Riots, the British began to reform local administration to create "proper" indirect rule in Eastern Nigeria. And a new local Native Authority Council and Native Court was introduced in 1930 but with modifications in structure from the formal one. It incorporated the elders and other local elites. The natives were now allowed to elect or appoint their own into the native courts and local councils. In 1947, Mr. Paul Ajah Onu of Ihuibe was elected as the only member of the native court from Okpanku. Jeremiah Obasi was elected by the people into the divisional or county council, and I joined him when Okpanku was split into two divisional wards. At this time, local councilors headed villages, while divisional councilors were elected to head wards and serve at the county council.

Years later, the government of Eastern Region abolished native administration and replaced it with the Local Council Ordinance of 1950. The Western Region followed in 1952 and the North in 1954. In the Eastern Region, the structure followed the British local government three-tier system of county/divisional council, district council, and local council. The ordinance made a provision that all members of the council be elected by the people. Because of inadequate administration and experience to run the three-tier local

• • • • • •

government system, it was further reduced to two: the urban or county council and the local or rural council.

Awgu County Council had divisional wards and local councils such as Okpanku Local Council, where I served as the secretary. At this time, the *Okaoha mma* or "Best Man" policy was in place. The British administration no longer used local natives as representatives of the people but encouraged the use of younger and educated members of the community.

Awgu County Council* was made up of the following communities:

1. Okpanku
2. Mpu
3. Ndeaboh
4. Nenwe
5. Oduma

The major committees of the county councils were:

1. Roads and Works Committee
2. Public Health, Education, and Scholarship Committee
3. Finance, Staff, and General Purposes Committee

County Councils also had council boards. For Awgu County Council, they were:

1. Awgu County Council, Cottage Hospital Board
2. Awgu County Council, Nenwe Secondary School Board
3. Sports Commission
4. Boundary and Land Disputes Board

These boards were created in accordance with the creation of the Local Council Service Boards in Southern Nigeria in 1955, to regulate the powers of the local authorities on the appointment of employees. In Northern Nigeria, the system was different since there were no council boards as the role was left to the approval of a government authority, say a regional minister.

I remain grateful to God for helping me serve with wisdom and

---

*Now Aninri Local Government Area in present-day Enugu State.

9. A Politician at 21

intelligence as a divisional councilor. I not only had advisers who helped me make decisions that benefited my people, but I also had enormous faith in God, believing Him to be the maker and finisher of my life. I had immense trust in Him, knowing that He would lead me to my expected end. I recall that on the morning after I was elected councilor, I re-dedicated myself to God, entrusting my new position in His able hands.

The prayer I said that day, as written in my diary, was:

> 1st Kings 3: 7–9. Now God, you have made your servant king in succession to David my father. But I am a very young man, unskilled in leadership. And here is your servant, surrounded with your people whom you have chosen, a people so numerous that its number cannot be counted or reckoned. So, give your servant a heart to understand how to govern your people, how to discern between good and evil, for how could one otherwise govern such a great people as yours.

This Bible verse became my anchor. I said this prayer every morning and night, especially amid great turmoil.

· · · · · ·

10

My Three Terms as Divisional Councilor

When my tenure as a councilor ended in 1961, I was elected unopposed to serve for a second term on September 4, 1961. This is because my people were deeply impressed by the zeal with which I went about my work. They saw that I never missed a meeting at the divisional council or failed to brief them on matters discussed there as it concerned them. They also recognized the mature and impartial way I handled cases brought to me as their councilor.

Before the expiration of my first term as a councilor, I moved a motion and lobbied the council into building a concrete bridge over the Ivo River. I was vice chairman of the Roads and Works Committee of the divisional council, so all roads within the jurisdiction of Awgu County Council were under my purview and supervision. I oversaw the maintenance of the roads and appointment of road laborers who cleared the bushes along the roads, and I also oversaw the building of culverts and bridges. Previously Ivo Bridge had been a death trap, as it was made with timber. Even when there wasn't heavy traffic on it, one took one's life in one's hands crossing that bridge. I took the Roads and Works Committee and the council's supervisor for works on a tour of the bridge. After this, they made a recommendation to the council that the bridge be built. The council approved this and forwarded this approval to the regional government, which then gave a loan approval to the council to build the bridge.

On November 26, 1960, the bridge was commissioned by the then minister of works of the Nigerian Eastern Region, Mr. P. O.

・・・・・・

10. My Three Terms as Divisional Councilor

Ururuka. This bridge would be blown up by the Biafran soldiers in July 1969, to stop the advancement of Nigerian soldiers.

Being a councilor came with challenges. It was not a lucrative job at the time, as the councilor would need to ride a bicycle (or trek to the council if he had no bicycle) to attend meetings. Then, he had to brief his people on the outcome of the meetings, organize them for events, and ensure the observance of law and order in his domain. If a crime was committed in the councilor's domain, then he was the first to be apprehended by the police. And when he failed to bring those involved to face the law, he was detained until they showed up.

During my three terms as councilor, I was a regular visitor at the police station, but one event that is fresh in my memory is a murder that happened in 1961. A man named Uguru Nteshi from Amaiyi Ikwo* was murdered by Stephen Akata, his kinsman. Stephen Akata allegedly eloped with and was living in a home in Okpanku with Regina, who was Uguru Nteshi's wife. Regina's husband searched for the duo for quite some time until he found them in the village of Egu Nkwo, where they lived in the residence of Mr. Joshua Okorie. He accosted Mr. Stephen Akata and a quarrel ensued, so Mr. Joshua Okorie ordered them out of his home and asked them to return to their community to resolve the matter. They all left Egu Nkwo late that night via Amaeze Road and were headed to Akaeze, where they were to get a lorry to Abakaliki. At a place known as Elu-iga along Amaeze Road, their quarrel reached a crescendo, and in the presence of Regina and Mr. Nwokpoke Agada, who accompanied Uguru Nteshi, Stephen Akata drew out his machete and killed Uguru Nteshi instantly. Regina ran back to Amaeze to alert Mr. Joshua Okorie, while Nwokpoke Agada ran to Akaeze, where he boarded a lorry the next morning to Abakaliki and reported the matter to the police. I went to the Awgu police station as the councilor to alert the police of this development, but I was immediately detained. Following police investigations, Stephen Akata was found where he was in hiding at

---

*Present-day Ebonyi State.

······

The Teacher Boy

Okposi and brought to face justice, and I was granted bail the following day.

My role as councilor was made more herculean by the fact that I was also secretary of Okpanku Local Council, a position I was elected into on May 24, 1961, and served in until 1964. It was another demanding position, which was like a humanitarian service to the community since it did not entail any payment or remuneration. The duty of the local council was to ensure that taxes were collected from the people, especially health and education taxes, and remitted to the county/divisional council. I was also the catechist of St. Paul's Catholic Church, Okpanku, and this came with its own demands, as I needed to be in church all the time to coordinate and lead Mass when the priest was not around, and to attend other church meetings and activities.

After my election into the council for the second time, the council convened on April 26, 1962, to elect members of various committees and the leadership of the council. I had already made friends during my first term as councilor and as the vice chairman of the Roads and Works Committee and had used that position to give my fellow councilors the opportunity to field their candidates as road laborers. I also gave approval for the construction of culverts, roads, and bridges in their domains, so I asked them to return the favor by supporting me to emerge as one of the leaders of the council.

Our people believe and understand that if the right hand washes the left, the left washes the right as well. So, I campaigned vigorously for the position of chairman for the Public Health, Education, and Scholarship Committee and got nominated by a councilor. Chief P. O. Mba and Mr. Emmanuel Eze were also nominated. But when the councilors cast their ballots, I won with 36 votes against Mr. Emmanuel Eze's 22 votes and became chairman of the committee. I considered this a rare honor and achievement because I was just a boy of 25. Most of the other councilors were men in their forties or fifties or even older men who were chiefs or had other respected titles. Most of them had more education than I did; I was just a teacher boy.

· · · · · ·

10. My Three Terms as Divisional Councilor

The committee was charged with the task of awarding scholarships to various colleges to deserving students under Awgu County Council. Our first assignment in this area was in December 1962 when the committee sat and awarded scholarships to students who were to commence their studies during the first term of the next school year of 1963. The first beneficiaries of the scholarship from Okpanku were

1. Louis Okereke—Corpus Christi College, Achi
2. Donald Nwosu—Corpus Christi College, Achi
3. Peter Chukwu—Corpus Christi College, Achi
4. Mark Ogbonna—St. John Bosco Secondary School, Ishiagu

Other students from other communities in Awgu County Council also received scholarships.

Next, I initiated the establishment of maternity homes in the three zones of Awgu County Council, and this was approved. Therefore, maternity homes were established at Mgbidi for Mbanano Zone, Owelli for Mbanabo Zone, and Ndeaboh for Egbo-etiti Zone. My committee employed nurses, midwives, security staff, and dispensary attendants for the three maternity homes. This impressed the leadership of the council immensely, and I was appointed the chairman of the Governing Board of Awgu County Council Cottage Hospital and the chairman of the Governing Board of Awgu County Council Secondary School, Nenwe. I was charged with the staffing, running, and maintenance of the school. I also employed more auxiliary teachers and cooks for the school as well.

These added positions came with more responsibilities, such that rest became impossible for me, for I was always on the road. Thank God I had a bicycle for my numerous trips and work. But riding a bicycle is not an easy job, especially when one has to navigate bumpy village paths and hilly unpaved roads. This was a hardship I had accepted with all my heart, however, and I was grateful to God to have been elevated above those who were older and more experienced than I was. I did not want to disappoint my family—my father

・・・・・・

The author during his days as a divisional councilor, 1959.

10. My Three Terms as Divisional Councilor

especially—or my community at large. I wanted to bring about development for my people, and I worked diligently for it.

Land disputes over boundaries became rampant around this time, and for each of them the councilor was summoned to adjudicate. Most times, a community dragged the other to a faraway town to report their grievances at a police station, necessitating that I travel to sort it out. In 1962, there was serious trespass by the people of Mgbom Okposi in present-day Ebonyi State on the Egunwko land belonging to the villages of Amaeze and Amagu of Okpanku. This trespass could have resulted in war and bloodshed, for the land was vast and attractive to both parties. Shortly afterwards, the Mgbom Okposi people, led by one Mr. Chukwu Eke, laid claim on a great portion of the land, insisting that the boundary was the *Iyi-nwa-eje* Stream and not the natural boundary known to all as Esu River. So, I began to collect opinions from elders of both villages, and, on February 2, 1963, I took 26 men from Mgbom Okposi to the native court at Ndeaboh for the trespassing case.

The case attracted the attention of such men as the then minister of education, Hon. Aja Nwachukwu, HRH Eze Solomon Chime Nkwo, Hon. Uneke Nwenyi, and other distinguished personalities from Okpanku and Okposi. The matter was decided to be resolved traditionally at the bank of Esu River. I was the representative of my people. I made my case, presenting the facts gathered from the elders, the survey map of the area showing Esu River as the boundary, and other documents, like the lease receipts signed by Mr. Chukwu Eke to allow them to plant timber and sell wood in Egunwko. The Mgbom Okposi people had no documents to tender. So, in a unanimous judgment delivered by Honorable Minister Aja Nwachukwu, the Esu River was reaffirmed as the boundary and the Mgbom Okposi people were pronounced guilty of trespass. They were ordered to relocate to their own side of the land, while Chukwu Eke and I were ordered to go back to the native court to inform them of their decision and to withdraw the matter.

In March 1963, soon after the judgment, I was accused of arson and dragged to the Abakaliki police station, where I was detained because of my attempt to drive the people of Mgbom Okposi from the land. The charge was later dropped by the police after they examined the facts of the matter.

Similarly, on March 9, 1964, a hunter known as Mr. Ezekiel Chienye from Isiukwuato, who lived with Jacob Uzoigwe in Amaeze Okpanku, shot and killed an Okposi woman while hunting in the Egunkwo forest. According to him, he mistook her for a monkey. After killing the woman, he ran and disappeared to his home community, Isiukwuato. I was arrested by the police, since I was the councilor representing Okpanku, and detained for two days until Ezekiel Chienye was arrested to face his crime. These constant arrests to answer for others' crimes were some of the many challenges that came with serving as councilor.

In 1965, I completed my second term as councilor. There was going to be another election. This time, more people had become interested in the position. They refused advice from the community that I be elected unopposed and argued that they were also qualified to serve. So, two persons indicated interest in running against me for the Okpanku II councilorship position. They were Mr. Festus Ukpabi and Mr. Abraham Ajaegwu.

One would expect that the demanding nature of the position would deter me from running for a third term, but this was not the case, for I had developed a love for the job, especially as it afforded me the opportunity to meet great minds from other communities who served as councilors. I believed in training and in knowledge building and cherished the training and workshops I attended as councilor. I also loved the respect that came with it and how I contributed immensely to bringing development and ensuring peace in my community. I wanted to continue to serve.

It was a tough campaign, especially since it was the first time I had been opposed, but I was equal to the task. In my years as councilor, I had made friends across the community, and I knew all the nooks and crannies of the community and understood the pressing needs of my people.

......

10. My Three Terms as Divisional Councilor

In fact, the campaign was so vigorous and treacherous that one day the local councilor for the village of Ihuibe invited me to his home, where he had assembled his people for me to address, saying he wanted me to discuss the modus operandi of my elections and the strategies I was adopting for campaigning in his area. But unbeknownst to me, one of my opponents was hiding in his inner room while we sat discussing in the sitting room.

Shortly after I left, someone ran after me and asked that I return. He informed me that my opponent was in the room all the while and heard all I discussed and promised. I rushed back to see that it was true. The village councilor was shocked to see that I caught him in the act. And when I told him to his face that he was a traitor and that he should keep all that I had given him for my campaign but not to bother working for me anymore, he felt like digging a hole in the earth and crawling into it. This was one of the early lessons in betrayal for me. I learned that it is difficult to ascertain what is in people's hearts and that politics is treacherous to the extent that men could go to great lengths of chicanery to achieve their selfish ends.

I had already painstakingly worked myself into the political bloodstream of the villagers. Of course, they were already like the biblical Adam and Eve who had tasted the forbidden fruit in the political achievements I had made and were not ready to let me go. They talked about my lobbying and diplomacy at the county council, which resulted in the construction of the Ivo Bridge and the scholarships I had secured for some of their sons.

The election was scheduled for April 26, 1965, and was to be held at St. Theresa's Catholic School, Amaeze Okpanku, but the electoral committee changed the venue to St. Peter's Catholic School, Ihuibe Okpanku, the village of my opponents. This change happened just two days before the election, yet people turned out *en masse*.

When the ballot was ready, Abraham Ajaegwu withdrew from the contest and Festus Ukpabi slugged it out with me. He was also a popular candidate from a well-known family. In fact, his elder brother had just returned from overseas as a professor and was ready to ensure that his brother won the election.

·······

The Teacher Boy

In the end, I was carried shoulder high as the winner of the election with 1,015 votes against Festus Ukpabi's 57 votes. It was a landslide defeat that shocked Festus and his brother, Professor Ukpabi. They could not believe it. The people not only voted overwhelmingly for me but also went on to issue a referendum and place their trust in me. This boosted my morale to soldier on in my determination to serve my people with all my heart—come rain or shine, even to my physical detriment—and to not succumb to easy wealth and life against the betterment of the people of Okpanku.

Four days later, the council convened for the leadership to be elected. I had become a tested and trusted politician, with immense knowledge of the treachery, shenanigans, and lobbying that went into the council elections. My only worry was that most of my colleagues who served with me in the previous elections were not re-elected; they had lost their positions to younger and more educated councilors. But the campaign system of the council was not new to me. I lobbied and got most of the new members on my side. I ran for the chairmanship of the Finance, Staff, and General Purposes Committee. Having served in the leadership of the other two committees, I wanted to serve in an area that was new to me and gain more knowledge.

The election was between me and one Mathias Chukwu. He won with 30 votes against my 28 votes. So, he became the chairman of the committee while I served as his vice.

In June that year, I decided to celebrate my success in the election and my emergence as the vice chairman of the committee with my people. I gathered my kinsmen from Umuogwudu Family for a party. It was also an opportunity to thank them for coming out *en masse* earlier in the day to help me stake my yams in my large yam barn. While we drank and ate and made merry, Mr. Festus Ukpabi and his younger brother walked in with an election petition, contesting my win in the April election.

What worried me the most was that the time for filing responses to the petition was to end in three days, meaning that the petition was dangerously delayed by my opponent. They had also

· · · · · ·

10. My Three Terms as Divisional Councilor

treacherously taken the matter to Owerri High Court, which was far from Okpanku, instead of Okigwe High Court or Enugu High Court.

But the test of manhood, says the Igbos, lies in one's ability to grasp the sudden. I assured my people that all was well. The next day, I got on my bicycle and rode to Akaeze Motor Park, where I boarded a bus to Aba in search of a lawyer; Aba was already a thriving commercial center with lots of reputable lawyers at the time. By the end of the day, two famous lawyers—Barrister P.K. Nwokedi and Barrister B.I. Metu—were recommended to me.

I did not know any of these lawyers or their skills in legal jurisprudence, but I quickly chose to work with Barrister Nwokedi. This decision was based on the literary translation of his name—"he who is a strong man." I had the feeling that my dignity hung in precarious balance, and the name "Nwokedi" was perfect for the situation. I was told that he was an expensive lawyer, but I did not mind. Barrister Nwokedi (now deceased) became my solicitor.

At this point, just one day was left for us to file our motions and respond to the petition. We quickly prepared them, and off I went from Aba to the High Court registry in Owerri to file. But there, I saw that the delay in serving me with the petition was about to repeat itself at the court registry. The registrar refused to see me. I waited in his office from morning until almost the close of work, without knowing that my political opponent and his brother, who was a professor, had gone to see him earlier.

Before the close of work, he asked his messenger to call me outside of his office. My heart was palpitating, as there was little time left. I did not know what he had in mind. He collected my petition and glanced at it, took out his red pen and marked it up, and threw the papers at me.

"Take it back to your lawyer," he said. "Tell him he is not serious."

I was in shock. *What did he mean that my lawyer was not serious?*

If I did not register and file my lawyer's response to the petition that day, I was doomed. I had no option but to rush back to Aba from Owerri in a taxi. When my lawyer heard what had happened,

· · · · · ·

The Teacher Boy

he told me that the registrar was compromised. He printed the same letter again, without any amendments since there was nothing to be amended. Then, he gave it to me and instructed that I should try to bribe the registrar's junior staff.

With only 30 minutes left to beat the deadline, I hurried back to Owerri. Instead of going to the registrar, I went to his junior staff, a clerk. He asked that I give him a bribe of £2 to accept my registration fee. I did. He took my documents, stamped them, and issued me a receipt.

Soon after, I heard the booming voice of the registrar call from his inner office, "Anybody else?"

I walked into his office and saw the surprise written on his face at seeing me. I gave him my file, and he saw that it had been registered. He was visibly angry.

"So, you, a small boy, are fighting with a professor? How do you think you will win?"

I said nothing. He insisted that I give him £5, though the file had been registered, before he would accept it. I had no choice but to give him the money.

My lawyer's first victory was to have the matter transferred from Owerri High Court to Okigwe High Court, which was closer to Okpanku, so I could afford to transport my witnesses to court. The journey to Owerri would have cost me a lot of money, especially the transportation and feeding of all my witnesses. In fact, if the matter had been heard at Owerri High Court, it would have been nearly impossible for me to afford it.

Surprisingly, the next court summons I received was for Okigwe High Court. This gladdened me.

There are rays of hope on the horizon, I thought.

The case suffered a series of adjournments, yet the petition and the case in court did not restrict me from serving as councilor. It did not stop me from attending meetings and discharging my duties.

On October 5, 1965, at Okigwe High Court, the very first election petition in Awgu Division was heard, and I was declared due winner of the election, with a fine of £50 against the petitioner.

· · · · · ·

10. My Three Terms as Divisional Councilor

My witnesses were delighted. I can never forget their sacrifices and efforts and how they stood by me through it all. Chief Ezekiel Chukwu Okereke was my first witness. Others were Mr. Okereke Aja, Mr. Michael Onu, and Mr. Mark Ogbonna.

When we left the courtroom, I gave some money to tax agents who were around and whispered that they should arrest Festus Ukpabi's witnesses. They quickly surrounded them.

I said to them, "You see, my witnesses and I pay our taxes. We are going home, but you people will be detained until you show your tax and rate receipts."

Even if they had paid their taxes, we knew that the chances that they would have their receipts and evidence of payment were slim. We wanted them to suffer for the stress they put us through defending the petition. They were visibly angry, wondering why the tax agents singled them out, leaving my witnesses alone. My witnesses and I went home, happily, mocking the others. It was the icing on our cake.

I served in the Awgu County Council until the military seized power in Nigeria on January 15, 1966, which saw the dissolution of county councils in the Eastern Region. The coup d'état started on January 15. It was organized by some majors in the Nigerian army and led by Chukwuma Kaduna Nzeogwu and Emmanuel Ifeajuna. Most of the coup leaders were Igbos, and from the day the coup took place, it was rumored both on radio and on the streets that it was an Igbo coup, though it has been written and argued that, at the time, the plotters had no Igbo agenda. The coup was executed based on the claim that those running the country were immensely corrupt. It did not help matters that an Igbo man, Major General Aguiyi-Ironsi, became head of state, replacing Prime Minister Abubakar Tafawa Balewa, who was killed. The situation was worsened as the Sardauna of Sokoto, Sir Ahmadu Bello, as well as some other northern and western elites, was also killed in that coup, while no Igbo leader was killed.

All through this period, I, like many others, was glued to my

・・・・・・

radio, constantly tuning the knob from one station to another to understand what was going on. Some of us feared that this coup was going to bring devastating consequences for the country. From that day on, tension began to rise. This would lead to the countercoup of July 1966, which killed Aguiyi-Ironsi and intensified the tension in the country.

Soon after, reports began to filter in that Igbos were being killed in the North, and pressure mounted on the military governor of the Eastern Region of Nigeria, Lt. Col. Odumegwu Ojugwu, to act. In our remote village of Amaeze Okpanku, people were whispering about terrible times ahead, but the situation was like when a cloud is heavy with rain but it is uncertain if or when this rain will fall. These coups and subsequent events led to the dissolution of the county councils. This dissolution was a blow to me, for it derailed all my efforts and political progress.

11

Second Marriage

The death of a loved one causes an ache in the heart that can linger and refuse to go. This ache burrows a hole in the heart, such that whenever that loved one is remembered, it feels as if a shovel is being used to widen the hole in the heart. This was my situation after I lost my first wife. Being a young man saddled with weighty responsibilities, I was always under immense pressure, juggling my work as a teacher, a catechist, and, most importantly, a divisional councilor. This pressure would have been assuaged if my wife were alive. After the day's work and the long rides on my bicycle to attend meetings, I would be sure that on my return, my woman would be there, readily available to ensure that I was comfortable.

Whenever my friends came to church with their wives or attended meetings or accompanied their wives to the market, I felt a pang in my heart. This pang was worsened by the circumstances surrounding Orieji's death, especially the burden that was placed on my shoulders as a young widower, immediately after she passed. The stress of that day—being close to her corpse, carrying it all by myself, and having to bury her—still remained a shock whenever I remembered it. It was always as if someone were digging a hole deeper into my heart.

These experiences, however, helped me build strong faith in God. I became a catechist in January of 1958, two months before Orieji passed. Before then, I had cultivated interest in God. I read my Bible diligently and participated in the teachings of the church with a strong zeal to know more about God. And I realized the ephemeral nature of human life and that the love of God outweighs what we can

The Teacher Boy

comprehend. I understood that most times He chooses to do things for a purpose that might not be clear to us but surely is for the greater good.

I also came to the knowledge that even though I lost a wife, God had also been good to me and had elevated me above many of my peers and contemporaries. So, I began to put my feelings of despondency in prayer, asking God to fill this hole in my heart. I prayed to Him to give me a new wife, someone who would understand me and raise my children in His ways. I prayed to Him to give me someone who would live with me until old age and share fond memories with me.

I also wished to marry an educated woman. My late wife, Virginia, was given to me by both our parents. Though she was a lovely girl who would have made a great wife, I knew that, this time around, I would need an educated woman who could complement me. I asked God to make this possible.

Not long after I committed into prayers this desire to have a young, educated wife who would build a home with me, I noticed a young girl in my class. I was working then at St. Paul's Catholic School, Okpanku, as a teacher. Her name was Patricia Uzoigwe from the village of Amabiriba, but she was fondly called "Patie" by her friends and family. She stood out because she was intelligent and beautiful and always neat. She was also smart and went about her duties and studies with a steadfast diligence that made everyone she came across admire her. She also radiated this ease and aura of one who was a free thinker and who could learn easily, adapt to any situation, and engage in meaningful conversation. She was a well-cultured girl who, despite her beauty and intelligence, had values that showed that she was well groomed.

I began to pay close attention to her, while praying over it. Then, I began to send her on errands, more than other pupils in my class, while paying attention to how she ran those errands.

It was 1959, and she was in Standard III. I knew I needed to take my time to watch her and to prep her. Of course, I was her teacher, so I had access to her every day and could tell a lot about her behavior, her thought process, and her conduct. I began to frequent her house,

・・・・・・

11. Second Marriage

to get acquainted with her family, and to know the kind of people they were.

Patricia was also good at sports. During small competitions, she represented the school in relay races. Back then, there was a special kind of race where the athletes ran with bottles placed on their heads, without the bottle falling off. She was good in this and represented the school at Awgu County Council, where she won. A similar race was the sack race, where the athletes put their feet into a sack while running, but this was mainly for boys.

On October 1, 1960, the day Nigeria gained her independence from Britain, the school organized a party for the teachers and the pupils. There was food to eat and drinks of all kinds. The students practiced and made drama and dance presentations to thrill the staff and parents who came to St. Paul's to participate in the euphoria of this new dawn. I watched keenly as Patie participated in almost all the activities that day. She was in the drama and dance and also was part of the march past.

Patricia Uzoigwe was born into a family of six. She had two older siblings and three younger siblings, whom she helped to groom. Back before she began studying and while in school, her younger siblings were entrusted to her care, and she was their nurse. I learned this from her and from her neighbors, while making inquiries about her.

Her father was a wealthy yam farmer, known for filling his barn with assorted yams of all sizes. He was titled *Ogbukere Gbusuo Agha*, a special name for one who had taken the horse title. In fact, not only had he achieved the title, but it took a long time after he did for another to take the chieftaincy title. He also had a war title, which in the olden days was taken only by strong warriors who went to war and returned with an enemy's head—though such wars had stopped. Wealthy and powerful men performed some elaborate rites that conferred upon them the same status as the men who went to war and returned with enemy heads.

I knew Patricia was loved by her parents because she was the only one of her siblings who was sent to school. Her two older siblings were not sent to school. Of course, back then, the elders saw the

・・・・・・

The Teacher Boy

education of a woman as useless, but her father loved her so much that he wanted her to get an education. So, she was enrolled in school in 1955. Her father had two more wives after her mother. This was because all her mother's three sons died, and he needed a son who would take his name and carry on his lineage.

Unfortunately, her father's second wife had no son at all. So, he married the third wife. She died during labor but birthed the baby before she died. According to Okpanku tradition, if the baby had died in her womb, it would have been considered a bad death and her corpse would have been thrown away at the evil forest. The baby, a son, was sent to a home for motherless babies at Ihuibe, but not long after her father got news that he had died. So Patricia's father had no son.

Her mother was also rich. At the time, women were encouraged to have their own wealth. So, she built wealth by farming, especially cocoyams, and achieved three powerful chieftaincy titles in Okpanku. The first was *Isi-ede*, a title reserved for women that required a woman to cook and invite everyone to her home to eat their fill. After this, such women were referred to as *Osiede*. Next, she took the *Igo-era* title. This meant she had paid her mother for breastfeeding her when she was born. It was a feast for one to honor their mother, and this cost a lot of money to achieve. She was also an *Ogbuefi*, for she had also taken the highest title for women. Therefore, Patricia's mother was an important, revered, and respected woman in Okpanku.

Patricia soon noticed the special attention I was giving to her. In no time, we became friends, and on June 3, 1959, I asked her to be my wife.

First, I wrote her a letter explaining my intentions, and she responded by saying, "Yes." She liked the idea. After that, I visited her home with the traditional gifts meant for expressing marriage intent, like two coconuts, soap, pomade, an English mat, and a sizable piece of meat for her mother. According to our custom, if the items were not returned four days after the visit, then Patricia and her family had accepted my offer.

. . . . . .

11. Second Marriage

The items were not returned after four days, so I was a happy man. I sang, whistled often, and walked boisterously. My heart was filled with happiness that God had answered my prayers and given me the chance to love again. Now, I was free to give her gifts.

I knew other students were jealous of her; this was obvious in their behavior. A teacher was an important person, and their classmate was not just going to be marrying a teacher but a catechist and a divisional councilor. Other teachers were also envious of me, for I had my eyes on one of the most intelligent girls in the school who was also from a good home and whom everyone was sure had interest in pursuing her education further than Standard VI.

Only a few girls had been to primary school back then. And other girls wanted to follow in their footsteps. The first was Rebecca Ivo Oti, followed by Margaret Udenwanyi Uzoigwe, and then Patricia's set of girls, which included Ada Janet Uzo, Janet Ewo, Udu Nwururu, and Juliana Anyim. But most of Patricia's contemporaries could not finish before they got married. It was only Udu Nwururu and Juliana Anyim who completed Standard VI with Patricia, making Patricia one of the first three girls to achieve that feat in Okpanku.

Patricia was in Standard IV when her parents accepted my proposal for marriage, and we began courting. At the time, it was common practice for a man and woman who intended to get married to court for some years. There were strict marriage rites that were followed. Before then, in the '20s, '30s, and '40s, it was the parents who found a wife for their son. The son had no say in this. The girl would be pointed out, and soon the family would perform the rites for their son. If they were from a wealthy home, the boy could have a wife found for him even at the young age of 10 or 12.

With education and civilization, most educated boys now found their own wives themselves, but tradition and customs were still followed. It was rare to see someone hold a marriage ceremony just a few months after he found a girl to marry. Potential spouses had to closely observe each other for some time, each investigating the history and lineage of the other's family before the union would be allowed to hold.

· · · · · ·

The Teacher Boy

Though I was Patricia's teacher and knew the kind of girl she was, I also wanted her to finish her primary education before I took her as my wife. So, we courted until 1962, when she wrote her Standard VI exams.

Something rather challenging happened in December 1961 that threw a wrench into my plans to marry Patricia. That month, placement slips for both secondary schools and teacher training colleges were released. I had sat for the teacher training college examinations, and when the result was released, I was offered admission to study at St. Paul's Teacher Training College, Awka. My younger brother, Louis Okereke, whom I was training in school, received admission into Corpus Christi College, Achi, for a five-year secondary education, and my fiancée, Patricia Uzoigwe, received admission to St. Joseph Teacher Training College, Aba, for a four-year course. As joyful as this was, I faced a dilemma.

The headmaster of my school, Mr. Christian Azimkpari, was married to Ude Nwanyi, who had completed her Standard VI in 1961, just a year before Patricia Uzoigwe. Ude Nwanyi was already working as a teacher in the school. The headmaster was happy that his wife and Patricia had interest in going for the exam. After they filled out their forms, they went for the exam at Okigwe. When the result was sent to the headmaster at school, he brought it to the school assembly and the letter was read. Patricia Uzoigwe had passed. She was the only one in the school who did. The headmaster's wife, Ude Nwanyi, did not score the cutoff marks.

Everyone was excited for Patricia. Other teachers congratulated me for making a good choice. I saw how Patricia grinned from ear to ear. Not long after, she went for the interview at Aba and passed. In fact, she came to ask me if she should go for the interview, and I told her that she should and gave her money to go for it.

My father, Okereke Abara, had become old and weak and no longer had the financial muscle to fund the education of my brother, Louis Okereke. In fact, I had been the one training him and seeing him through school, so if Louis was to go to Corpus Christi, his education was to rest solely on my shoulders. I also had to finance my

・・・・・・

11. Second Marriage

own education and, most importantly, that of my wife-to-be. Because I had expressed interest in marrying Patricia, it meant that I was the one responsible for her upkeep and further education, if she wanted to pursue that. This was a puzzler.

Who would go? This was the question on my mind that caused me sleepless nights.

I spent days tirelessly in prayer, asking for God's intervention and for him to provide me with a solution to this problem. It was during this time that I discovered Psalm 121:1: "I lift up my eyes to the mountains, where is my help to come from? My help comes from God who made heaven and earth."

I sought advice, and my fellow teachers advised that I send my wife to school. She was going to be the first woman in Okpanku to go to teacher training college. They argued that she was going to be my wife, the one who would spend the rest of her days with me, and that if she had a TTC certificate and got a job as a teacher, then life would be easy for me as a family man. Some advised that I send Louis since he was a man and would need education to navigate through life. They told me that it was his trust in my ability to fund his education that gave him the courage to buy the entrance form for college.

I went to meet the man acting as the middleman for my marriage project and talked him into helping me convince my future father-in-law to allow me to send my brother to school first, with the assurance that I was going to take care of his daughter and ensure that she went to teacher training college later. This man was a close friend of my future father-in-law's.

Teachers at my school began trying to convince my fiancée not to go along with my plan. They even went as far as telling her that if I insisted on not sending her to school, then one of them was willing to take over from me, marry her, and send her for the training. One of the teachers even went as far as writing Patricia a letter, wooing her, and informing her that if she agreed to marry him, then he was going to fund that education. Only two women were educated past Standard VI at that time; they were Salome Ogwo and Professor Sampson

······

The Teacher Boy

Ukpabi's wife, who was already in the university then. These teachers told Patricia that she could be like these highly revered women.

Finally, I made the decision to send Louis to college. I reasoned that if Louis did not go to school, he was going to amount to nothing. When Patricia became my wife, she would live with me and we could work things out, and if Louis completed his studies, then I would be in a better position, financially, to send her for further studies. So, on January 5, 1962, I went to the market in Okigwe Township with Louis' college prospectus and bought the materials that he would need to go to school.

Louis was visibly excited. He was an intelligent chap with the desire to pursue education and had feared, when he saw that my fiancée and I had gotten admitted as well, that he might not be able to fulfill his dreams. But I made the sacrifice for him, dropping my own ambition and Patricia's to ensure that he could pursue his dream.

A few days after, Louis was escorted to Awgu by bicycle, and from there he boarded a lorry to Corpus Christi College, Achi.

Patricia was unhappy that she was not going to go to teacher training college that year. This bothered her so much. She was visibly sad and decided to break off the engagement, but I persisted. I recall that my morning devotion on June 28, 1963, came from Exodus 34:10: "I am making a covenant with you. Before all your people, I will do wonders never before done in any nation in all the world. The people you live among will see how awesome is the work that I, the Lord, will do for you."

Armed with the assurances in this verse, I believed in God that Patricia would become my wife. And before sunset of that glorious morning, my father and some of my relations returned home with Patricia, having gone to her father's house, according to tradition to fulfill the necessary rites. They returned to shouts of joy. She had become my wife. It was one of the happiest days of my life. Volleys of gunshots rang out and neighbors gathered to join in the merrymaking and to welcome the new bride with gifts, songs, and dances.

Consequently, on August 3, 1963, Patricia and I wedded at St. Michael's Catholic Church, Awgu, under the holy hands of the

· · · · · ·

11. Second Marriage

Reverend Father T. Buckley, the parish priest, and with Mr. and Mrs. Mark Chukwurah as sponsors/witnesses. Barely four months after, on December 20, 1963, my dear father joined his ancestors on a journey through that cave from which one never returns to earth.

12

Sy de Moon Is Disengaged

It was 1964. I was a 27-year-old man, recently married and juggling family life with life as a politician. By now, Sy de Moon had become the name by which I was most often called. I became a councilor at 21, got re-elected, and served in various positions.

I had been a teacher for several years and loved my work immensely. So, I ensured that I was in school every day, not missing any classes. This was in spite of the fact that, in addition to being a councilor, I was chairman of Awgu County Council's Public Health, Education, and Scholarship Committee while serving my second term from April 26, 1962, to April 24, 1964. I was also a member representing Awgu County Council at the Sports Commission of Eastern Nigeria Wrestling Association up to January 31, 1964, and had just been made a member of the Tax Assessment Committee for the communities of Okpanku, Mpu, and Ndeaboh, where I served until 1967.

My love for teaching outweighed all these other opportunities and obligations, including the trainings and workshops I frequently attended. My students liked me. Other teachers were happy to work with me, and most headmasters I worked with valued my input and leadership experience. I was a respected figure in Okpanku and in the entire Awgu Division. Therefore, one can understand how I felt in December of 1964 when I was disengaged from teaching.

All auxiliary teachers were summoned that fateful December morning to Awgu by the Reverend Father McGreen, the reverend manager in charge of the Catholic schools. We were addressed and informed that we had been disengaged and were served with papers

······

12. Sy de Moon Is Disengaged

of termination. We were to be replaced with newly trained teachers who had just graduated from teacher training colleges.

The letter of disengagement became as heavy as a bag of stones in my hand, and when I put it in my pocket, the bag of stones weighed my pocket down. Several times, I took it out to look at it. Though I was no longer a councilor, having finished my second term on April 24, 1964, the end of my term did not bother me as much as losing my teaching job did. I was going to miss my students, their laughter and their childish idiosyncrasies. I was going to miss my physical education classes, the games and sports, and the early morning preparation for my lectures. It was a situation that put me in an awkward position. Several times, I attempted to board my bicycle for home but hesitated. I did not know how my wife was going to take it. We had barely been married for one year. Finally, I summoned enough courage and got on my bicycle and began the long journey back home.

On my way, while riding, the events of 1962 came to mind, the hard-nut-to-crack situation when I had gotten an admission offer to pursue my Teacher Grade II certification at St. Paul's Teacher Training College, Awka, and I had sacrificed it for my brother Louis to go for his college education at Corpus Christi College, Achi. I also thought about my wife's admission to St. Joseph's Teacher Training College, Aba. I wondered if not sending Patricia to school was a mistake. I knew for sure that if I had pursued further education, I would not be in this situation. These thoughts rode with me for the long journey to Amaeze Okpanku. Before I got home, however, my mind was calm. I had made the sacrifice for my brother, and there was no sacrifice one made for family that was not worth more than gold.

Several days later, while these thoughts weighed me down, I remembered an Igbo saying: "When a White man is disengaged from work, he might commit suicide, but when an Igbo man is disengaged, he picks up his hoe and machete for farm work." I decided that this disengagement could be a blessing in disguise and an opportunity for me to try other things while I waited to gain admission to pursue my education, for I was determined to go back to teaching at some point.

・・・・・・

The author and his wife, Patricia Okereke, during their visit to the United States of America.

12. Sy de Moon Is Disengaged

A friend directed me to Aba to see a man from the village of Amaogudu in Okpanku who was working with the Electricity Corporation of Nigeria (ECN) at the time. He suggested that it was possible this kinsman could help me get a job with ECN, owing to my vast experiences.

It was a good suggestion, I thought, and I decided to give it a try. A few days later, I left for Aba.

The man I was referred to was named Mr. Johnson Okorie, popularly called Dumoke. He was a technician with the company. In fact, he was more than a kinsman, for we shared some extended family relationship. His father was the brother of Ivo Okorie, one of Ogbu Abara Okereke's wives. When I introduced myself to him, he was more than delighted to know that we shared blood relationship. He told me that he was going to do everything within his power to secure an appointment for me with the company, as there were existing vacancies at the time. You can imagine my joy. For me, working with the company would give me another opportunity to grow my skills and experiences in that field, which at the time was a new area for me.

Mr. Johnson Okorie demanded my credentials and an application letter and asked that I give him the sum of £20. I thanked him and left for Okpanku to consult with my people. As I now had a wife, I believed that most decisions were best discussed with her. That way, I would be sure that I was making the right decision, for two heads, they say, are better than one. When I discussed this with my wife and my mother, my mother confirmed the relationship. We agreed that since he was a relation, he would not betray me. I left for Aba a few days after with copies of my credentials and the money. At the time, £20 was a lot of money, especially for one who has just lost his source of income.

Mr. Johnson Okorie took me to the controller of ECN, Aba Zone, a Yoruba man, who confirmed, to my delight, that vacancies existed. He liked my credentials and was impressed by my résumé. He gave me a date to come for the interview, about two weeks hence. I returned home with hopes of success in getting this new and lucrative job.

・・・・・・

The Teacher Boy

A day before the interview, I left for Aba to be sure that I did not miss it. Mr. Johnson Okorie was surprised to see me come a day early. He told me that the interview had been canceled. What I did not know was that he had used the money I gave him to pay the rent on his house. I went to the ECN office to ascertain the next date for an interview, only to see those who had gone for the interview leaving the office. I went in to see the controller and told him what had happened.

He said, "Igbo people cannot be trusted. Your brother refused to comply and did not bring the money. Get out of my office!"

I was devastated by the betrayal by my kinsman, Mr. Johnson Okorie. I went back home to my village and decided to go into farming, for there was nothing left for me to do. I was not one to fold his hands and do nothing when faced with a challenge. I had seen and experienced a lot in life to learn that at every challenge, one must find a ray of light and go for it, though it might be hard. But it was better to try and fail than to do nothing.

With the help of my wife, I started cultivating yams and cassava on my father's tens of acres of land. It was a herculean task, which was physically demanding and mentally draining, but we soldiered on, under the sun and in the rain. With the death of my father, I had become the head of the family and had my mother and my father's other wives to feed. I also had my stepsiblings and Louis to see through school. I oversaw their welfare and was the one everyone went to when they needed money or medical attention.

One of the challenges that came at this time and shook me to my bones was that, shortly after I started cultivating my farms, a terrible storm came and brought along with it a heavy flood that eroded my farms and crops and pulled down people's houses including those of Njoku Onu, Njoku Ugo, Ajah Onu, Onu Mgbo, Njoku Chukwu Njoku, and Samuel O. Chukwu of Ihuibe, to mention but a few.

This was another perplexity. How was I going to start again as a farmer? I was sure that there was no running away from farming, since my family and I must eat, but my efforts had been washed away by the marauding flood. I had to wait until the next planting season.

・・・・・・

12. Sy de Moon Is Disengaged

The only option left for me was to wait and start all over the next year. This meant that my family could go hungry. I did not want to beg anyone for food; nothing would make me do so. I thought long and hard and decided that, for the time being, I would go into trading. I was not one to be idle or laze about. While serving my people in various capacities, most of which were unpaid, I needed to provide for myself and my new wife and for my family.

I negotiated for a building at Ogwumabiri Market to open a provision store. Peter Mba, a man from Mkporo* who resided at Amaogudu, rented one of his lock-up shops to me. I went to Awgu and purchased a patent medicine license and off liquor license. Equipped with these licenses, I journeyed to Aba with the help of Ngagha Oji, a well-known trader who sold his wares only on Afor market days when the market was sure to be filled with people from everywhere, and bought all that was needed to stock the shop. But I was going to use a different approach; my shop would be open every day, not just on Afor market days.

I stocked the shop with provisions of all kinds, including books, utensils, biscuits, matches, kerosene, and lamps. Another section of the shop had medicine, soft drinks, beer of all varieties, and soft drinks of various kinds. I recruited one Ferdinand Obasi to be my clerk, and business began.

I continued trading these items, keeping my body and mind busy and providing for my family and other needs, until a new farming season when I would go into aggressive yam and rice farming.

I leased a vast rice swamp from Mr. Makwe Ubani and Okorie Uzoigwe, both from the village of Amagu, and got two other portions of land from my great grandfather and father's lands at Egu Nkwo forest. This time, I ventured into farming with great enthusiasm. With the money I made from trading, I paid laborers on my yam and rice farms. Not long afterwards and over several years that followed, my produce so increased in bounty that all the village's women used to organize themselves repeatedly to go to my farm to help bring

---

*Present-day Abia State.

••••••

The Teacher Boy

back my harvests, in line with the communal help system that was in place in those good old days.

For my farm, I adopted some modern methods such as the use of fertilizers and pesticides. The application was right and timely, as I had attended several agricultural workshops in the past. People soon came to my farm for practical lessons. I had become a great farmer, and if I had wanted, I could have taken titles. In Okpanku tradition, a farmer is known to be great when he takes such titles as *Ike Ohu*, *Ohu-la-eri*, *Mazi Inyinya*, and so on, and could also perform such titles for his children. When a man wanted to take any of those titles and did not have enough resources, he could pledge his farmland to a wealthy farmer who would support him with a supply of enough yams needed for the title ceremony. If the loan was not repaid after the agreed upon time, the pledged land would be forfeited. Farming, especially yam farming, was important and respected work, and it was celebrated with the *Ikeji* Festival. During the festival, farmers sent yams to their in-laws. This gesture was also extended to the orphaned and widows.

Since my yam and rice farms were doing well and I had become somewhat renowned and successful, I expanded my operation to include a palm plantation. I figured that the palms would become a permanent moneymaking venture since they would bear fruit and be processed yearly for several years to come. So, I went to a place known as Agu-enyi in the community of Mpu to a man named Mr. Nwa Germany who dealt in palm trees and citrus fruits. There, I made purchases of young palms in batches on the following dates as follows:

  11-04-1964 = 62 local young palms
  15-04-1964 = 130 local young palms
  17-04-1964 = 60 local young palms
  19-05-1964 = 20 local young palms

These palms were purchased at the cost of £1 each. On June 13, 1964, I purchased five orange trees from Chief P. O. Mba, and on June 18 I bought three more. On September 17, I bought two young kola nut plants from him.

······

12. Sy de Moon Is Disengaged

I also secured land at Ogwumabiri and built a six-room mud block house in 1965, for my own provision shop, medicine store, and a restaurant to be managed by Mrs. Comfort Ohawgu. It was the first restaurant in Okpanku. My store attendants also increased; I employed Christopher Elechi and David Nwafor as clerks. Soon, I became one of the first persons to build a cement brick house of six rooms in Amaeze; it is still standing today. For my leisure and pleasure, I got a brand new Philips radio set, which was magnificent to behold, such that whenever I turned it on, people hurried to come dance to it.

Looking back to those good old days now, I am filled with nostalgia for what I was able to achieve with the help of my lovely wife, Patricia, despite the odds that were stacked against us at the time and the challenges we faced. I realize that whatever one sets one's mind to achieve, with determination, is possible. It is a testament that my life would have turned out differently if I had succumbed to despair when I was let go from my job as a teacher.

· · · · · ·

13

My Time as a Farmer

Just like teaching, farming and trading gave me immense joy. Even though they were difficult ventures that required time, hard work, and attention, I loved them and devoted all that I had—my attention and energy—to them. I divided my time between my trade and my farms. In the mornings, I would wake up early and head to my farm with my laborers, and in the afternoons, I would return to shower and go to my shops.

I had learned bookkeeping while at Ishiagu as a Standard VI pupil. Those experiences and knowledge became useful. I taught my clerks not only how to keep proper accounting but also how to run the shops. So, my clerks were doing well.

During my third term as councilor, a European named Mr. Gibbs came from Onitsha Province to address us about a project known as the Oil Palm Rehabilitation Scheme in one of our meetings. It was on December 5, 1965. He explained what this project was and said that land was needed for it; vast unused land was identified in Okpanku, Mpu, and Oduma. Councilors from these three communities were asked to indicate if they were interested. When we stood up and announced our interests and the benefits it would bring to our people, Mr. Gibbs took my particulars as well as those of Chief L. A. Ukpai, who was paramount chief at the time, representing Okpanku at the Awgu County Council.

When we got back to Okpanku, Chief Ukpai and I, along with the other councilor, Jeremiah Obasi, summoned all taxable adults in Okpanku and informed them of the development. We told them of the benefits of using our land to plant palm trees. The palms would

······

13. My Time as a Farmer

be communally owned by the people of Okpanku after they were planted. The Europeans were also going to supply us with fertilizers for the project. The people were excited. All the villages in Okpanku agreed to surrender a part of their land for the project, pending Mr. Gibbs's assessment of which parcels he thought fit for the project.

The following Saturday, Mr. Gibbs came to Awgu County Council to be sure the people agreed. The councilors gave their feedback, and dates were given for Mr. Gibbs's visits to each community. Months after, on March 20, 1966, he came to Okpanku. The people trooped out *en masse* to listen to the White man. They were excited to see him. Mr. Gibbs thanked them for embracing the project and explained the economic benefits the palm trees would yield for the community. He informed us that an agricultural extension agent was to be assigned to us who would select a suitable site for the project and help to ensure that it succeeded.

As Mr. Gibbs was concluding his speech, we saw a crowd of women and men marching toward us with leaves and sticks. We were shocked to see that they were protesting the project. These protesters had been rallied by some men including Dick Makwe, Okereke Chukwu, Chukwu Aja, Chukwu Eru, Paul Ivoke, and Fredrick Aja, to mention but a few. They had campaigned around Okpanku against the project and had mobilized protesters. They were shouting at the top of their voices that the paramount chief and I had sold Okpanku land to the White man for lots of money.

"Shame on you!" they cursed.

Some of them approached and spat on us. Some threw sticks at us.

The elderly among them hit their staffs on the ground, saying, "We thought you were honorable people!"

All of this happened to the utter disbelief of Mr. Gibbs. He was flustered, for he knew that it was impossible for any single individual to claim ownership of the project or to take the selected lands as his own, so he hurried away. When he got to Awgu County Council, he left a letter giving instructions that palms and fertilizers should be dropped at Ndeaboh and be shared by the agricultural extension

・・・・・・

The Teacher Boy

worker-in-charge between Sylvester Okereke and Chief L. A. Ukpai. He figured that since the community did not want the project, he would give it to us, and we could own the palms and have them on our own lands.

Some community people were not in support of the show of shame demonstrated by the protesters, yet no one was called to answer for it or to give account before the community for what they had done even though the law stated that if one had been shamed publicly in a matter where they were innocent, the custom demanded that they be given public apology.

When I was informed that I now had loads of palms and fertilizers at Ndeaboh waiting for me to pick up, I summoned a meeting of my *ikwu* and informed them of the development. I did not know what to do with the palms, I told them, for there were a lot of them.

One of the elders of my family, Mr. Ogbu Chukwu Itata, said to me, "My son, if you had killed a mighty animal, say a buffalo, we would have come to share it with you. Now that this one is trouble, it is right that we do not leave you to bear it alone, for you have not committed any crime and everyone knows this. The Okereke Obasi family will give you, our son, land to plant your palms."

His position was supported by others. Mr. Chukwu Okereke mentioned two parcels of land that I should be given and added that he feared that I might die, but if I had the courage, I could enter the family's *ajofia* at Onu Ogidi and I could clear it and plant my palms. Joseph Abara, my uncle, and David Okereke supported this, saying that if the two parcels of land I was to be given were not enough to plant the palms, then I could use the bad bush. They said that they were sure nothing would happen to me, since I was a Christian.

Buoyed by their support but still anxious about this turn of events, I went to Ndeaboh on May 10, 1966, for the palms. The agricultural officer, Mr. Edwin Azuokwu, shared the palms between Chief Ukpai and me, and we both got 900 palms and 25 bags of fertilizer. He gave me my Agric number—OP/EN/AG39A—and a date to start working on planting the palms.

I rode from Ndeaboh to the parish at Awgu to meet with the

......

13. My Time as a Farmer

parish priest. There, I discussed with him my fear of entering the bad bush. I was his catechist, and he had immense respect for me. He strengthened my heart and told me that there was nothing to fear. He told me that it was humans who referred to the forest as the bad bush because it was used as a common graveyard but that nothing devilish or fiendish was wrong with it, and I had nothing to fear. He assured me that he would come himself to pray over the land, and if there were any evil spirits lurking about, then he would drive them away with his prayers. I was encouraged by his words.

On May 16, 1966, the priest, the Reverend Father T. Buckley, came to my village to support me just as he had promised. I took him to the bad bush. He said his prayers and walked around the land, sprinkling holy water while I held a lit candle. When he was done, he told me to start my work and be afraid of nothing.

On May 18, 1966, the agricultural officer came, measured out the land into parcels, and pegged it. At first, I could not find laborers, for no one from Amaeze agreed to set foot on the land, including members of my *ikwu*, the Umuogwudu family. Finally, I hired two Akaeze men—Mr. Choke Ajali and Mr. Kalu Ezeoke—who lived in Amaeze to work for me. Choke Ajali went to Akaeze, his community, and brought more laborers, and they were accommodated in my house.

When we began planting the palms, we realized that the two parcels donated by my family and the bad bush were not enough for my share of 900 palm trees, and I went to Ogbu Chukwu Itata for advice. He was sympathetic and took me to his land, a small portion of land at Ogwu Aviaekpa. I bought this land from him for £5.10. I also spent £1 for *nri ali*, a customary rite performed after buying another's land to bestow its ownership on the new buyer. I bought four pots of palm wine, four kola nuts, and two shillings' worth of tobacco, all to go with the customary rites. Because I spent money buying the land from him, paying laborers, and working on the lands, and due to the high cost of transporting the palms and fertilizer from Ndeaboh, I could only bring back 510 palms; the only readily available means of transportation was bicycle. I left 390 palms

· · · · · ·

The Teacher Boy

and 10 bags of fertilizer at Ndeaboh. After planting the 510 palms, I worked extra hard to secure the palms from fire and animals, as this was also one of the conditions subject to approval by the extension officer.

The next year, 1967, when Afikpo and Amasiri were invaded by Nigerian soldiers, I was able to hire some people who ran to Amaeze as refugees to work on the farm at a reduced cost.

Despite all the dire challenges and efforts made to ensure that the palms were not wasted, some descendants of my kinsmen who supported my palm plantation project turned against me years later. The first challenge came 13 years and two months after I planted the palms on both the bad bush and the two parcels of land gifted to me by my family. Several litigations followed as well over the next few years. But, in all, I am happy that other kinsmen were given portions of the family land to plant their own palm trees, though with different outcomes depending on how well each looked after their own.

······

14

The Nigerian-Biafran War

Following the coup of January 1966 and the events that culminated in the killing of Igbos in Northern Nigeria and with the government of Yakubu Gowon not being able to do anything about it, tension was rife. It was the worst of times, and no one knew what was going to happen the next day. It was difficult to sleep with both eyes closed as Igbos displaced by killings and riots in the north began returning to Eastern Nigeria in droves.

With shadows of the uncertainties of the January 1966 coup cast over everyone, robbers invaded my shops on January 31, 1966, and took away as much cash and portable articles as they could carry. They left the stores nearly empty. When I got there, I did not know what to do. For me, it was as if at every turn, when I tried to make progress, some challenge would come to attempt to knock me down. Running a business that sold cheap articles as provisions and medicines came with little profit, just enough to make ends meet and sustain myself and my family. A robbery as I had suffered was enough to make one bankrupt, but over the years I had built myself up to face adversity. Starting from when I was sent to faraway communities to live with unknown families at a young age, to the difficulty in accessing Western education, to the death of my first wife, to my travails as divisional councilor, I had been prepared by fate and circumstances to shoulder heavy responsibilities. So, I knew that these challenges were steppingstones to greater heights. I picked myself up and gradually replaced the things stolen from my stores.

At this time, Igbos were returning from the north in the tens of

The Teacher Boy

thousands. Those who returned came with gory stories that made one's skin crawl. The tension and the inability of Yakubu Gowon's federal government and the Eastern Region to find common ground caused Odumegwu Ojukwu, who was the military governor of the Eastern Region, to announce the secession of the area under him from Nigeria on May 30, 1967.

Things became worse. On July 6, 1967, General Yakubu Gowon, who was the head of the Federal Military Government in Nigeria, declared war on Biafra, and all hell broke loose. The Nigerian army began the bombardment of the Biafran areas. We saw military jets and planes fly past on several occasions. The radio carried news of deaths across various towns, and, not long after, refugees from the Anambra area began to arrive in Okpanku. In early 1968, when Afikpo fell, the number of refugees doubled. These refugees were camped at St. Paul's Catholic School, Okpanku. The school hall was where they retired to sleep at night. Some of these refugees had sustained serious injuries, and most were sick, including children and women. When a person died, the body was dumped in the school field until a grave could be dug. It was a gory sight.

In February 1968, Okpanku was invaded for the first time by a troop of soldiers crossing from Oduma to Arochukwu. On their way, they burned houses in many villages in Okpanku, especially Amaogudu, where they stopped for a while. They also burned houses at Amabiriba and Ihuibe, but none was burned in Amaeze. It was a terrible attack that left some people dead; I was lucky not to have witnessed this first attack, as I was away from Okpanku. While the war raged, I was faced with another strong concern. My younger brother Louis had a serious health challenge that had added another hefty load on my shoulders, and I had taken him to a hospital in Orji River as the war was starting. When the fighting became heavy in that area, I traveled to Orji River amid heavy risks to bring him home.

As the war raged around us, Louis's health continued to deteriorate. This gave me cause to venture out of Okpanku. After weighing my options, I figured that it was better I took the risk than watch him die in his prime. I decided to take the risk, and on February 6, 1968, I

・・・・・・

14. The Nigerian-Biafran War

took Louis to a hospital at Uzuakoli.* He was admitted immediately. It was while we were at Uzuakoli that the attack happened.

Many people in the affected villages, including Amaeze, had escaped and relocated with their families into the forests. But my family, especially my young wife, was worried. She did not know what to do. When they did not see me, they feared that I might have been killed. They did not run away with the others. They were waiting for my return.

On my return, I saw that Akaeze had been attacked. The Nigerian soldiers who took Afikpo had started shelling and advancing into Akaeze. Houses were burned and property destroyed. The story on everyone's lips was that Okpanku had been invaded by Nigerian soldiers, and the situation was the same. Men were being sought to be conscripted into the army, and houses were being destroyed. The Biafran soldiers were feared as much as the Nigerian soldiers. Fearing that the road was not safe, I entered the forest into Amaogudu farmlands. I followed the bushes until I got into Amaeze and entered my home. It was a terrible journey since, at this point, it was not the fear for wild animals that ate at my soul but that of machine guns and shelling.

The next morning, when the situation worsened, we packed up what we could. I took my first two children, Nneka and Gregory, and my wife, Patricia, who was breastfeeding our third child, Celestine, who had been born just four days before. Together, we made our escape into Uburu. With us were my father's other two wives and their children. We escaped into the forest and through it got into Uburu. My mother was the only one who remained with my sister, Monica, at Amaeze. Monica had just gone into labor, but her placenta had refused to birth. There was no way Monica could manage the mile walk. My mother said that she was not going to leave her behind and if the war was going to kill her daughter, then it was better they died together.

The people of Obegu Uburu refused to accommodate refugees

---

*Present-day Abia State.

The Teacher Boy

and asked that we enter the inner villages. I refused because we knew no one in the inner villages of Uburu, and I feared that they might suspect we were saboteurs and maltreat us. So, we relocated to Owere-ebu, in Egu Nkwo forest, an Amaeze farm at the boundary of Amaeze and Uburu. It was a forest area, and we presumed it was safe.

It was difficult living in the forest, especially as we had a few-days-old baby in our company. We quickly dug out the earth, pounded the soil, and began to mold it to build a house in this forest. Then, we made a fire at the four corners of the house so that the heat and smoke could dry the wet mud quickly as the building construction progressed. Luckily for us, that year we had farmed at Owere-ebu and our farms were located not far from where we made our new homes in the forest, so we could harvest whatever we could.

Many other families came into the forest to establish makeshift homes as well, and not long after, the place became a small, nucleated village settlement, hidden by bushes such that it was difficult for any invading army or military jets to see that people were settled there. When it was time for another planting season, we replanted what we could, including yams and cocoyam.

Not long after, the men summoned courage and entered Amaeze to peep into the village and see what was happening. There were a few people in Amaeze who did not escape into the forest or into other communities. It was from them we got regular information about what was going on.

While we were hiding away at Owere-ebu and the war was raging, the Biafran army entered Okpanku on May 22, 1968, and made it an occupied outpost. They camped at Mr. Sunday Ogwudu's house and many other homes in Amaogudu and turned my stores into their preferred resting place. They entered the stores to collect whatever they needed without paying a dime. Had the clerks said anything, they would surely have received beatings; they feared for their lives. My own life as the owner of the shops was not safe either. I had to order that the stores be closed.

The next year, on August 26, 1969, during the war, a storm with heavy rainfall destroyed buildings in Okpanku. The mud house I had

• • • • • •

14. The Nigerian-Biafran War

The author and his wife, Patricia Okereke (second and third from left), with their first daughter, Nneka Okereke (left); their son, Chukwumerije Okereke; his wife, Boma; and their children, David, Ruth, and Rachel, during a welcome-to-the-USA reception and the celebration of Patricia's 80th birthday hosted by Nneka Okereke in Maryland, USA, in 2017.

erected not long before with proceeds from my farm work and business was destroyed. It was a lawless time; thieves took away whatever they could lay their hands on from the fallen building, leaving only a few of the remaining zinc roofing sheets and wood, doors, and windows that they could not carry.

On September 22, 1968, the Nigerian army invaded Okpanku through Akaeze. They burned down houses and killed people and animals that crossed their path. They caught peoples' goats and took them back to their camp at Akaeze. Two days later, Okpanku elders organized themselves and went with gifts to Akaeze, where the Nigerian military had camped, to pay allegiance to them and plead that their community be spared.

Old men and women died in droves because of shock due to the death of loved ones, loss of property, burning of houses, and shelling

· · · · · ·

The Teacher Boy

and sounds of machine guns. People were buried quickly when they died.

On January 20, 1969, Nigerian soldiers returned to Okpanku and burned some houses, which led to the death of Sunday Makwe, who was burned while in his house. The Nigerian soldiers set up a permanent camp at Akaeze. They also burned one Ukpani Ogo's house, and his mother died in the fire; his house was burned because they knew through their informants that Biafran soldiers had camped in that compound. On May 26, 1969, Nigerian soldiers killed four Okpanku men, and on July 5, 1969, Uzoigwe Uneke, who was Okpanku's representative to the Nigerian army at Akaeze, was shot at night by Biafran soldiers from Oduma Camp who claimed he was a saboteur to the Biafran cause.

That same sad day of July 5, 1969, members of the Biafran Organization of Freedom Fighters (BOFF), which was a special guerrilla warfare and special operations unit of the Biafran army, made up mostly of civilians, including women, blew up the Ivo Bridge, to ensure that they forestalled the advancement of the Nigerian army.

At the time, the BOFF was a strong and useful arm of the Biafran army. One of their notable members at the helm was the acclaimed writer Chinua Achebe. Their members were trained in sabotage, to infiltrate enemy lines, and to ensure that if the Nigerian military occupied any captured Biafran land, then they were cut off from their other divisions. The BOFF team, which blew up the bridge, was led by an Arochukwu man named Mr. Moses Akpaeru who was living at Mpu before the war.

Some Okpanku men who understood Hausa switched sides and worked with the Nigerian military against the Biafran cause. They were known as saboteurs. One day, as the war was winding down, I went from the Owere-ebu forest to mend the roof of my house at Amaeze. There, some Nigerian soldiers came and surrounded me. They were in the company of Ukpai Makwe.

"Come down! Come down!" they ordered.

"Yes sir. Yes sir," I whispered, trembling and fidgeting. My heart had sunk into my stomach.

・・・・・・

14. The Nigerian-Biafran War

They ordered me to take them to the home of one of them known as Obasi Aliewu.

"Run along!" they commanded me.

I jogged all the way, while they walked behind me. Trembling on shaky legs, I took them to Obasi Aliewu's home, but they did not see him. They told me that if they came again and they did not see him, then they would burn down the entire village and kill everyone in sight. After the soldiers left, I ran back into the forest. After the war, these Okpanku men who were referred to as saboteurs—Obasi Aliewu, Abraham Ajaegwu (who withdrew for me during my third-term election for divisional councilor in 1965), and Ukpai Makwe—became the most feared and influential people in Okpanku.

Louis visited us at our hideout in Owerre-ebu forest, saying he came to see if there was money to get. How he had managed to get to Amaeze at this time was bewildering. Things were hard, and money was an essential commodity; it was like gold and difficult to come by. What he wanted was £4.4. I was able to squeeze out all we had to give the money to him.

By December 1969, it became obvious that Biafra would fall. Most of the area that made up the new country had fallen. Many radio stations reporting on the war aired different stories as it suited them. What Voice of America was reporting differed from the news on Radio Nigeria, and Radio Biafra's story was different from the reports from the British Broadcasting Corporation.

On Christmas Day of 1969, news circulated that the war was over. Though the war had not been announced to be over, it was obvious that it was going to end soon. Okpanku people gathered at the Ihuibe village square in jubilation, but Nigerian soldiers came from Akaeze and opened fire, killing scores of them. It was a terrible sight, a devastating incident. These were defenseless citizens whose crime was to gather to celebrate that the war was soon to end and, for the first time in three years, celebrate Christmas. Bodies were thrown one atop another as people were shot at different points of escape. Men were shot in the head, on the neck, buttocks, and legs. These

• • • • • •

bodies had to be given mass burial; at that time, the dead were buried quickly without any funeral or ceremonial rites.

By the next month, it was obvious that the war was over. And on January 11, 1970, it was reported that the Biafran leader and commander-in-chief, Emeka Odumegwu Ojukwu, had left the country for the Ivory Coast. The next day, news was rife that Biafra had surrendered, and Col. Philip Effiong announced a surrender that same day, January 12, 1970. On January 15, 1970, the Nigerian military head of state, General Yakubu Gowon, officially declared the civil war over and received a surrender note from Col. Philip Effiong, who was second-in-command to Chief Odumegwu Ojukwu and became acting head of Biafran State on January 8, 1970.

· · · · · ·

15

Back to School

After the war ended in 1970, life was hard, at first, for every Igbo person. There was a government policy, announced by General Yakubu Gowon, on the advice of his then minister for finance, Chief Obafemi Awolowo, that everyone should pay into the banks any Biafran currency they had. We paid in all we had and received just £20 in return. No matter how much you paid in, you only got back £20.

This policy worsened the hunger, poverty, and inflation in the Eastern Region, especially for those who lived in the urban and semi-urban areas. For me, who resided in a rural village and had not stopped farming, even during the war, I was left with no other option than to see the continuous growth and sustainability of my family. I had to go back into farm work with increased intensity and vigor. I knew, without being told, that the survival of both my immediate and extended family was dependent on me. I was no longer a teacher or a divisional councilor, so the only way of making ends meet was farming.

By the end of 1974, my efforts and hard work had paid off. I had more than enough to show for my farm work. My yam farms stretched for miles on end, and it took several people to haul my produce home after every harvest. I also completed an eight-room cement block house in my compound; I was the first among my age group to achieve this feat.

By early January 1975, five years after the war, things were almost back to normal. Businesses started to thrive again. Schools had picked up, and the academic calendar was restored. A teacher, Mr. Innocent Mbubu, was transferred to St. Theresa's Catholic

······

The Teacher Boy

School, Amaeze Okpanku, from Orlu in Imo State of Eastern Region. Recall that St. Theresa's School was the one I brought to my village of Amaeze to make education accessible to my people. I had also accommodated teachers for free in my home. So, I gave one of my rooms to Mr. Mbubu.

One evening, while we were having a conversation, Mr. Mbubu impressed upon me the need to further my education so I could go back to teaching. He advised me to enroll for teacher training to enable me to obtain my Teacher Grade II Certification.

"I would like you to consider the future of a teacher and compare it with that of a wealthy farmer," he said.

I thought about this. Though I loved teaching a lot, I had grown to love farming as well, and it came with a lot of wealth, more than I could get from teaching, though the work involved was more.

"As a farmer, you might be rich, but have you considered the fact that you will age some day and by then you will have no energy to engage in farm work? As a civil servant, the more you age, the more your rank rises such that at retirement, you are sure of your pension and gratuity," he told me. "You should consider going back to teaching. When you have higher education, it comes with other opportunities besides teaching, of course."

He urged me to seek to regain my teaching appointment, and few days later he came home with a copy of *Outlook Newspaper*. I saw the heading on the publication: "Examination into Teaching Profession in Eastern Region." The date fixed for this examination was January 20, 1975, and the testing centers were all listed in the paper. He again kick-started a conversation about the need for me to go back to school and obtain a TCII, but I told him that I had dropped my paper, pen, and chalk on December 31, 1964, almost 10 years before, and did not know if I still had it in me to study and teach.

"What will I write in an examination?" I asked him.

Mr. Mbubu told me that he knew I was an intelligent man and that if I set my mind to it, then there was nothing I could not achieve. I discussed with my wife, and she agreed with him. So, I decided to give it a shot.

・・・・・・

15. Back to School

On the morning of January 20, 1975, I left home on a bicycle to go to my examination center, which was at St. Michael's Catholic School, Awgu. I met other candidates from Okpanku who were indeed surprised to see me come for the same examination. No one would have thought that now being a wealthy farmer, a politician, and retired auxiliary teacher, I would still have interest in teaching. Behind my back, some of them made jests, saying that they were sure I would not know what to write. More than 500 candidates were present for the examination.

The results were published in *Outlook Newspaper*, and to my surprise and delight, I saw my name listed as one of the successful candidates. The interview was fixed for February 20, 1975. After this interview, I was successful as well and was re-engaged as a "C Teacher." I was posted to what was formerly St. Paul's Catholic School, Okpanku. The name of the school had been changed after the war to Central Primary School, Okpanku. It was no longer under the management of the Roman Catholic Church.

Having learned my lessons in the past when I was disengaged from teaching and had no source of income to fall back on, I did not leave farm work but combined the two. But I was conscious of the time invested in farm work, as I had taken the decision to study to be able to write an examination and enter teacher training college, so that I would not be laid off again. To ensure that I got back in shape in my profession, I dropped some of my friends with whom I had formed the habit of going to Akaeze, almost every weekend, to hang out at beer joints for recreation.

I enrolled in evening lessons with Mr. Cyprian Aja and Mr. Innocent Mbubu, who taught me different subjects to prepare me for teacher training. On my own, I drafted a home study timetable, which I followed strictly.

In 1977, an opportunity came for examination into teachers training colleges. I was sure that I would do well if I sat for the examination, having equipped myself within the space of two years with evening lessons and self-study. I passed and was posted to study at the then popular St. Charles Teacher Training College, Onitsha,

· · · · · ·

The Teacher Boy

which was famously dubbed "University on the Niger." Mr. Anthony Chukwu Ukpai and other Okpanku teachers were posted to TTC Ihe-Awgu and St. Paul's TTC, Awka. Mr. Anthony Chukwu Ukpai and my political mentor, Chief Lawrence A. Ukpai, who were both posted to Ihe-Awgu, advised that I switch to TTC, Ihe-Awgu, as Onitsha was far and costly.

I thought about it and said to them, "Our people say that if one needs quality products, then they go to Onitsha Main Market. It means that good things are at Onitsha." So, I made up my mind to go and to brace myself for whatever challenge would come with this decision.

The author (right) and his friend during their days at St. Charles Teacher Training College, Onitsha, in the early 1980s.

By January 1978, all preparations were concluded for my re-entry into school. I dusted off my books and dropped the habits of sniffing tobacco snuff, which I had picked up the day Virginia passed, and drinking bottles of gin and beer. I was now ready and prepared for the life of a student.

During registration, I met the principal, Mr. B. I. A. Okafor. It was indeed a small world. I was delighted to meet this man. When he asked my name and I told him, he looked up at me, smiled happily, and shook my hands.

"Do you know me?" he asked.

15. Back to School

"Of course I do," I responded.

He looked me up and down and tried to test my memory. "Where do you know me from then?"

"I was your boss when you were principal of Awgu County Council Secondary School, Nenwe. Then, I was the chairman of Awgu County Council's Public Health, Education, and Scholarship Committee and by extension the chairman of the Board of Directors of that school."

He said that was true and was both surprised and elated to see me. We chatted for a while, and he was surprised that I had no further education other than Standard VI when I was a divisional councilor. He was also indeed surprised that I was an intelligent and hardworking astute politician who was heading such a big office at the time. He was also happy that I chose to further my education and to not leave the teaching profession. He said he knew that my experiences in life, especially in politics, would benefit students, especially young people. He had immense respect for me.

After school commenced, the principal, to my greatest surprise, called me out amid old and new students and the school staff during school assembly. He announced that he had made me the senior disciplinarian of the school. It was the first time in the history of the school that a freshman would be made senior disciplinarian. I served in this office from January 1978 to July 12, 1980, when I graduated.

This was a new role for me. I worked with the teacher in charge of discipline in the school, and he led me through the process of handling the senior students in the school. The senior prefect of the school was from Awgu Local Government, just as I was. His name was Mr. Paul Okeke, and we teamed up. I drew up a schedule that would enable me to study and discharge this new responsibility. The schedule blocked off time for receiving students' reports, handling students' problems, and studying.

My daughter, Nneka, was admitted into secondary school the same year I started studying at the teacher training college. It was difficult communicating with her, and this was challenging for me. I also missed my wife, Patricia, as Onitsha was far, and it was impossible to travel home often or when I wanted. Then, there were money challenges, for whatever I made from farming went into caring for my extended family, seeing my children through school, and my sustenance at Onitsha. To augment what I had, I left the school on weekends and went from one residential home to another, asking if there were menial jobs or farm work to be done. I got some of these jobs and made a little cash. It was difficult at first as this kind of situation could bruise one's ego. It was also difficult knowing that I was once a divisional councilor for three terms and had served in various capacities, but these difficulties did not deter me. I knew that they were temporary challenges and if I checked my ego and did everything I could, then I would soon become victorious. I also developed serious catarrh, arising from dropping tobacco snuff abruptly, so I went to a hospital in Onitsha and spent some money to receive treatment.

Not long after, I was posted to a school in Onitsha for teaching practice. This became another challenge, for I had no money most of the time for transportation or food. I trekked to the school, most times, and on an empty stomach, but I had a clear vision of where I was going. Nothing could stop me. Other students facing similar challenges withdrew, but I refused to succumb to failure. If I succeeded as a young boy sent to live in strangers' homes while in primary school, I could also do well as an adult.

The school had strict rules and regulations on punctuality to classes and morning assembly; this did not help my situation. Students were also to attend morning devotions. They were to appear neat or be dismissed. Students could keep their hair short or grow it, but if it was bushy and unkempt, they received two weeks suspension. The student was expected to go to Onitsha Main Market to buy a razor blade in the first week, which he had to bring to school after the second week of suspension to have his hair shaved off. After this, the senior disciplinarian would take the erring student to the principal for re-admission. Students were mandated to dress in the school's day dress even outside the school for easy identification. The principal was known to say: "If you pass through St. Charles, allow St. Charles to pass through you."

· · · · · ·

15. Back to School

By January 1979, after I had been in the school for one year, the principal announced that the federal government would conduct an examination for "C Teachers" for an honorary Grade II Certificate Award, on a local government basis. He asked that those willing to sit for the examination come forward, so he could sign their exit cards. Students who were qualified did and left the school for their local government areas. I had no money to travel, so I approached some students who were my friends and borrowed from them.

The examination was held at Holy Rosary College, Enugu, and after the exam, I used that opportunity to visit home to see my family. Results were released in March 1979, and I passed. I then had the choice: I could leave St. Charles with an honorary Grade II Certification and lessen my hardship and burden or face the next year and graduate with a Meritorious Grade II Teachers Certificate. I gave this some thought; others might laugh at me and say that I had just an honorary certificate. I also thought that if I dropped out, the years spent studying at St. Charles would have been wasted. So, I continued at St. Charles. This time, I became more active in school activities, especially in athletics. And in 1980, I graduated with a certificate of merit in extracurricular activities. While at St. Charles, I served as the chairman of Awgu Student Union from February 1978 to July 7, 1980. The principal noted that, with my help and efforts, the school recorded the best student leadership in the school's history.

Posting After St. Charles College

After my training, I was posted to Community School, Amaeze Okpanku, formerly St. Theresa's Catholic School, Amaeze, in September 1980. The headmaster of the school then was Mr. Vincent Udeobasi. I was to teach Elementary V. I resumed teaching at the school with new vigor and teaching methods, and the school headmaster, staff, and pupils loved this new way of teaching that I learned from St. Charles College. It soon became common for students from other classes to leave their classrooms and come to mine to enjoy my

• • • • • •

The Teacher Boy

lessons, especially during physical exercises and games, which were my favorite. I was the teacher who oversaw labor, games, sanitary, and discipline.

To leave a mark at the school, I successfully traced and marked the school boundary with sticks all around to discourage trespassers. I also got the community to repair dilapidated school desks and chairs. Then, I donated footballs regularly in pairs, one for junior pupils and the other for senior pupils. I also built a volleyball pitch for the girls and taught them how to play the game. I also took over paying for the education of five less privileged pupils.

In December, a letter was sent to the school transferring me out. When Mr. Simon Onyeabor, who was the headmaster then, read it, all the students in the school started crying. Their cries attracted the attention of parents, who ran from their homes into the school to find out what had happened. On learning that I had been transferred out, they staged a protest, which involved the entire community. They wrote a letter of protest and forwarded it to the education secretary at Awgu, and the transfer was reversed.

This incident left an indelible mark and impression in my heart and deepened my love for my students and for teaching. I put in more effort. I knew the names of all the students, not just those in my class but in the entire school. And in the community, I became known as Teacher Okereke, a name that has remained popular.

On January 8, 1985, I was posted to Community School, Amagu, under the headmastership of Mr. Fredrick Osita. I was appointed assistant headmaster and placed in charge of games, labor, and handwork. I formed a school committee to help secure the boundary of the school and farmed around the school boundary to stop locals from encroaching into the school land. I also used proceeds from the sales of the handwork the students produced to purchase most of the things the school needed, every term.

I initiated and organized a football competition between the two community primary schools in Amaeze and Amagu and rallied the community to build a five-classroom block and a school latrine for boy and girls at Amagu. Between January 8, 1985, when I was posted

• • • • • •

15. Back to School

The author with his pupils during a physical education class in his days at St. Charles Teacher Training College, Onitsha, in the early 1980s.

to Community School, Amagu, to December 31, 1992, when I retired as a teacher, I awarded scholarships to four pupils.

Though I have since retired from teaching, I am delighted in the knowledge that my students have become great persons in society. I am proud to have been their teacher every time I encounter them. Among the students of whom I am proud are HRH Igwe Cyprian Ije; HRH Igwe Augustine Ani; Hon. Jonas Ogbuagu; Mr. Charles Eze, who is a university lecturer; Hon. Chief Emmanuel Eze; Mr. Felix Okoro, an urban surveyor; Sgt. Paulinus Okoro; Late Chief D. A. Okoro; Late Chief Ignatius Ojengwa; and Mr. Donatus Uzoigwe.

Every day, I see that my life is filled with God's blessings, and I know that one person God has used to take control of my life and to provide the necessary stability is my wife, Patricia.

She is one of the greatest gifts God gave me. She agreed to marry me despite the challenge at the time regarding sending my brother, Louis, to school instead of her. And though I sent him instead of her, she never begrudged me this or showed any animosity to Louis.

· · · · · ·

The Teacher Boy

The author and his wife, Patricia Okereke, during a welcome-to-the-USA reception and the celebration of Patricia's 80th birthday hosted by Nneka Okereke in Maryland, USA, in 2017.

Patricia understood and remained committed to me and to our marriage. She also never gave up on her dream of becoming not just a teacher but a trained one at that.

When I decided to apply for teacher training college, she gave all her support. Around that time, we planned that while I was at school, she would care for the family and run our affairs, especially the farm and our business, and after my graduation, she would then

· · · · · ·

15. Back to School

get into school. I got into the college in January 1978, and on February 3, 1978, Patricia got employed as a teacher and was posted to Community Primary School, Amaeze Okpanku. It was one of the best moments of our lives, for she was going to become an academic, which had always been her dream.

Patricia took her job seriously, and whenever I had the opportunity to return from Onitsha, she told me of all her teaching experiences, especially with her students and other teachers. She showed that she was an exceptional woman, for she did not allow the farm or our family to suffer any setback in my absence and was able to shoulder all the work and responsibilities with efficiency—doing extraordinary things that only a few women could do, especially at the time.

Immediately after I graduated in 1980, Patricia was admitted into Women Training College, Enugu, which was one of the prestigious schools for women at the time. We, therefore, succeeded in structuring our lives such that we achieved our individual goals of pursuing our education despite financial challenges and the setbacks of juggling studies with caring for our children. While she was in school, I was available at home to care for the family and take over the responsibility of running our farms again.

Patricia graduated from Women Training College, Enugu, in 1984 with flying colors and became a Grade II Teacher. She was the envy of other women of her mates and age-grade at the time. Patricia continued to teach, attending trainings and finding opportunities to grow her skills and teaching abilities. Her zeal to have more education never wavered. She enrolled for a National Certificate of Education and graduated in 2009. And in 2012, she retired as a head of personnel management. Since then, she has continued to provide support for schools in Okpanku in any way she can.

Patricia is a virtuous woman who made every effort to complement her husband and provide the needed anchorage for our family and me in the times of need, stress, and crisis, especially standing by me since we got married. Her life and personality make me aware of how blessed I am to have her as my wife. And the older we get, the more I agree with the saying, "The older the wine, the better."

• • • • • • •

16

Sojourn into Eze's Court and Customary Court

One of the district officers of the Old Awgu Division, Mr. Orlando Peter Gunning, shows in his historical background report that the Eastern Railway Line from Port Harcourt was started in the year 1913 and reached Enugu in 1916. He reported that Ndeaboh Native Court was built in 1916 and comprised the communities of Mpu, Okpanku, Oduma, Ndeaboh, and Nenwe, all under Okigwe District Court.

Warrant chiefs served as judges under the Native Court Administration. Chief Paul Aja Onu from Okpanku was the last warrant chief from Okpanku to serve as a judge from 1947 to around 1957. Native courts, now renamed customary courts, were again introduced in Nigeria in 1993. Following this introduction, I was the first customary court judge to represent Okpanku. I served as a customary court judge from October 1993 to June 2014. But before my sojourn into the customary court as a judge, I had also gained experience in the court of the king's palace, first as the Eze's secretary and later as a chief.

Becoming a Secretary/Member of the Eze's Cabinet

Following the setup of the local council system in the Eastern Region of Nigeria and the abolition of warrant chiefs, a law was set up to establish paramount chiefs to take charge of communities. This system was modeled after the kingship system in place in western and northern Nigeria.

......

16. Sojourn into Eze's Court and Customary Court

Consequently, Mr. Lawrence A. Ukpai was unanimously elected on December 10, 1958, as the first paramount chief of Okpanku. By the new law, Chief Lawrence Ukpai was co-opted into Awgu Divisional Council. He joined Mr. Jeremiah Obasi and me, already elected in September of 1958, barely two months before. At the time, the chief had no cabinet but had the power to receive complaints and disputes and dispatch them accordingly. He also attended both local council and divisional council meetings.

With the new chief, Jeremiah Obasi and I organized frequent monthly meetings of leaders, elders, and village councilors to discuss problems facing the community and development issues, and worked to limit court litigations. During the civil war, the local council and paramount chief system of government were dissolved. And the communities were left with no ruler or leadership. Later, a law was set up establishing the traditional council system, putting an end to the paramount chief system of government.

By January 1977, seven years after the civil war, a general meeting of the community was held to elect a traditional ruler. But there was no existing constitution or guideline to follow. So, a committee of seven members, one drawn from every village in Okpanku, was set up. Also on the committee were three elders from every village. To ensure that the committee met its obligations, the community needed someone with experience and respect to drive the set agenda, and I was chosen as the chairman of the Chieftaincy Constitution Draft Committee. The following served as members:

Chief Francis O. Agwu—Vice chairman—Amaogudu village
Mr. Patrick C. Okorie—Secretary—Amabiriba village
Mr. Edwin O. Aro—Assistant Secretary—Amagu village
Mr. Patrick A. Njoku—Member—Okpu village
Mr. Daniel Chukwu—Member—Ihuibe village
Mr. Moses Okoroafor—Member—Uhuezeoke village

The committee got to work immediately under my leadership, and on February 20, 1977, a general meeting of Okpanku was called to review, amend, and sign the constitution. An election for a new

The Teacher Boy

king was also slated for March 20, 1977. Three candidates stood for that election: Chief Lawrence A. Ukpai, the last paramount chief; Ambrose Ivoke, a retired police inspector; and Festus O. Chukwu, former personal assistant to the minister of education. Election officers came from Awgu Local Government Council, and after the voting, Mr. Festus O. Chukwu was declared the winner. He was installed as the Eze Oha I of Okpanku on March 31, 1977, and was presented to the district officer by the people.

The new king showed that he had gained a lot of administrative experience while working with the federal minister. He set up his cabinet and appointed me his first palace secretary, a position I held from 1977 until I left for further education training at St. Charles College, Onitsha, in 1978.

When I returned from St. Charles College, Onitsha, in 1981, the Eze, HRH Festus O. Chukwu, brought me into his cabinet as a chief. He had a council of chiefs who advised him on cultural and traditional matters and every other issue that came up at his palace. Aside from adjudicating disputes and promoting peace in Okpanku, the king mobilized the community through communal labor, and a bamboo bridge was put up across Ivo River to help pedestrians to cross easily, as the other bridge that was blown up during the civil war was yet to be repaired.

In this dispensation, many of the bridges and culverts damaged during the civil war along Okpanku-Akaeze and Okpanku-Mpu roads were reconstructed. This was done by introducing mass work in all the villages to maintain the roads, especially during rainy season. Already, there was a challenge of attending meetings outside Okpanku or even attending the community's central meetings at Amabiriba Central School because the king's car could not cross Ivo Bridge.

On March 2, 1984, the Eze, Chief Festus O. Chukwu, passed on at Uburu Joint Hospital and was laid to rest in his palace on March 17, 1984.

On September 17, 1989, five years later, the community unanimously elected Mr. Reginald Aja Chukwu as the second traditional

・・・・・・

16. Sojourn into Eze's Court and Customary Court

ruler of Okpanku, and he became the Mkpume Asaa I of Okpanku. Chief D. C. Uzoigwe was elected a traditional prime minister. This was done after the constitution was amended. This king set up a bylaw guiding the Eze's cabinet and followed in the footsteps of the first king, his predecessor. He attracted the attention of the government, and a cottage hospital was built in Okpanku. He also mobilized the women of the community to use the money collected at their annual August meetings to build a residential quarter for doctors at the cottage hospital. This building was completed and handed over to Aninri Local Government Council. He was the first in the local government to have women serve in his cabinet, which was a

The author during his visit to the United States of America.

・・・・・・

welcome development, as it promoted equality of both genders and encouraged other women to work hard in the society. He worked to ensure that Okpanku High School was built and completed in 1994 and introduced Community Self Development Project, which brought electricity to Amabiriba, Amaogudu, and Amagu—and electricity poles to Amaeze.

The Eze worked hard to promote farming by giving incentives and presents to deserving farmers during new yam festivals in a competition involving all interested farmers in the community.

On January 27, 1996, I was selected by the Umuogudu kindred and elected by the village of Amaeze as a chief in the Eze's cabinet. At the time, I was already a customary court judge who served as adviser to the king and his cabinet. After a six-year term, my time at the cabinet as a chief expired, and I was re-elected to the cabinet on April 1, 2009, and have been there since. While serving on the cabinet, I brought my rich knowledge of the cultural and traditional practices of Okpanku to bear, and they were found so helpful by the king that I always accompanied him as chiefs' representative to meetings at the local government headquarters. Together, we have stood behind various villages in the community in land disputes and in difficult times.

My Time in Okpanku Local Council

On May 24, 1961, I was elected as secretary of the Okpanku Local Council. It was also the year I was elected to serve for a second term as divisional councilor and the year my planned marriage to Patricia could have suffered a stumbling block because of my decision to send Louis to school instead of Patricia. As a member of the leadership of the local council, I worked hard with others to ensure that taxes were collected for education and health and to ensure that we worked to ensure peace and development in Okpanku.

Part of our achievement at the time early in my tenure in the local council was to build a dispensary between Amabiriba and

・・・・・・

16. Sojourn into Eze's Court and Customary Court

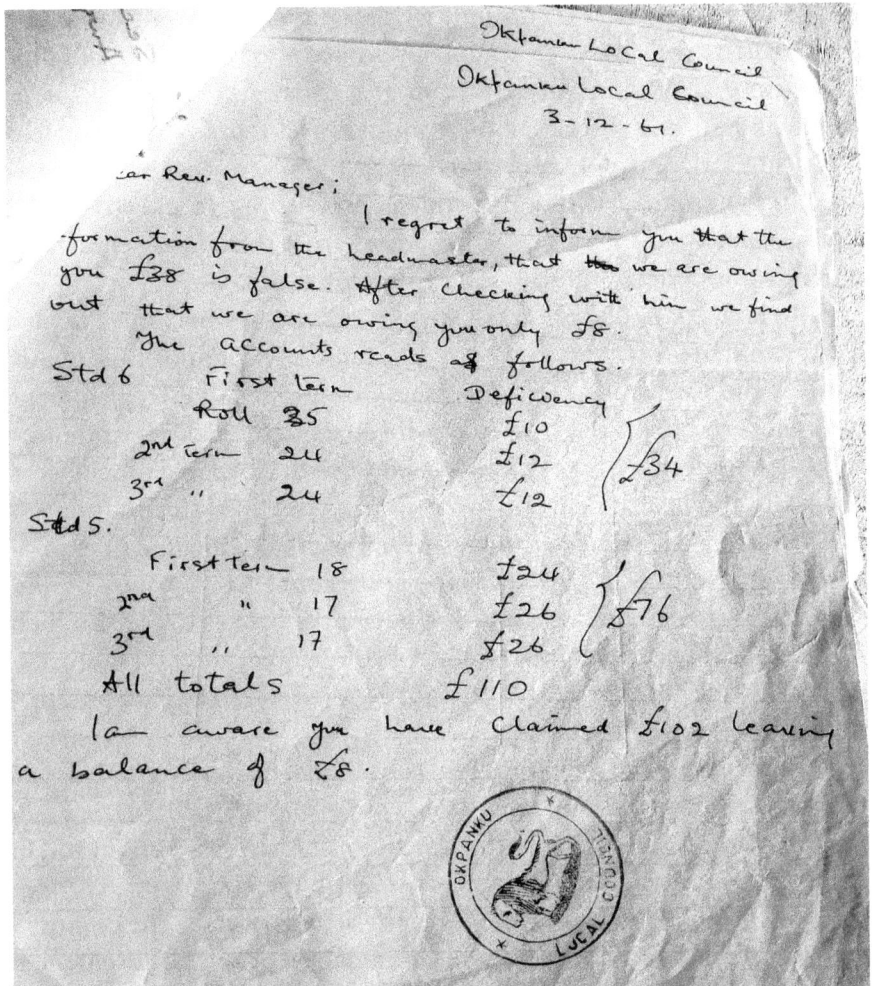

A letter to the reverend manager of Awgu County Council about the Assumed Local Contributions by the author when he was secretary of Okpanku Local Council in 1961.

Amaogudu. This dispensary was built under direct labor; it became the first medical facility in Okpanku. After the dispensary was built, it was handed over to Awgu Divisional Council for staffing and maintenance. The building was destroyed during the civil war, and the landowners took over the land afterwards.

· · · · · ·

The Teacher Boy

While I was in the council, we attracted the attention of the then Ministry of Health to send health officers for treatment of guinea-worm diseases and eradication, and those infected with communicable diseases such as tuberculosis and leprosy were sent to hospitals for treatment. I worked hard to ensure that we encouraged healthy sanitary living, encouraging Okpanku locals to dig pit latrines and assisting sanitary inspectors from the county council to move around the community on inspection tours.

By January 2000, when the former dispensary became a health center managed by the local government, I was appointed chairman of the Committee of Okpanku Comprehensive Health Center. I worked hard to ensure that villagers accessed the hospital for treatment and that doctors, nurses, and Youth Corps members were posted to the health center. The committee secured the boundaries of the hospital with hedges and ensured the employment of Okpanku natives as staff. I was also made the assistant secretary of Okpanku Youth Movement, and we worked to adjust the bylaws to control such issues as bride price in Okpanku, the riding of bicycles and motorcycles without lights at night, and fighting or stealing at Ogwumabiri Market.

There was the need to reconstruct roads, culverts, and bridges damaged during the civil war. This was initiated by HRH Eze F. O. Chukwu, who had become the paramount ruler of Okpanku. He embarked on the project in partnership with Okpanku Youth Movement and Okpanku Town Union. I was asked to oversee the committee set up for the reconstruction of damaged bridges and culverts along Okpanku/Akaeze Road. I did this job satisfactorily, and lorries soon began to access Okpanku for farm produce and give the people easy access to the rest of the world.

In February 2000, I was made the chairman of School-Based Management Committee for Okpanku High School. It was common knowledge—and it still true today—that if anything is to be done in the area of education in Okpanku, I must be involved, owing to my high level of experience in the education sector. I decided that for things to move fast, we had to use community labor to overhaul

······

16. Sojourn into Eze's Court and Customary Court

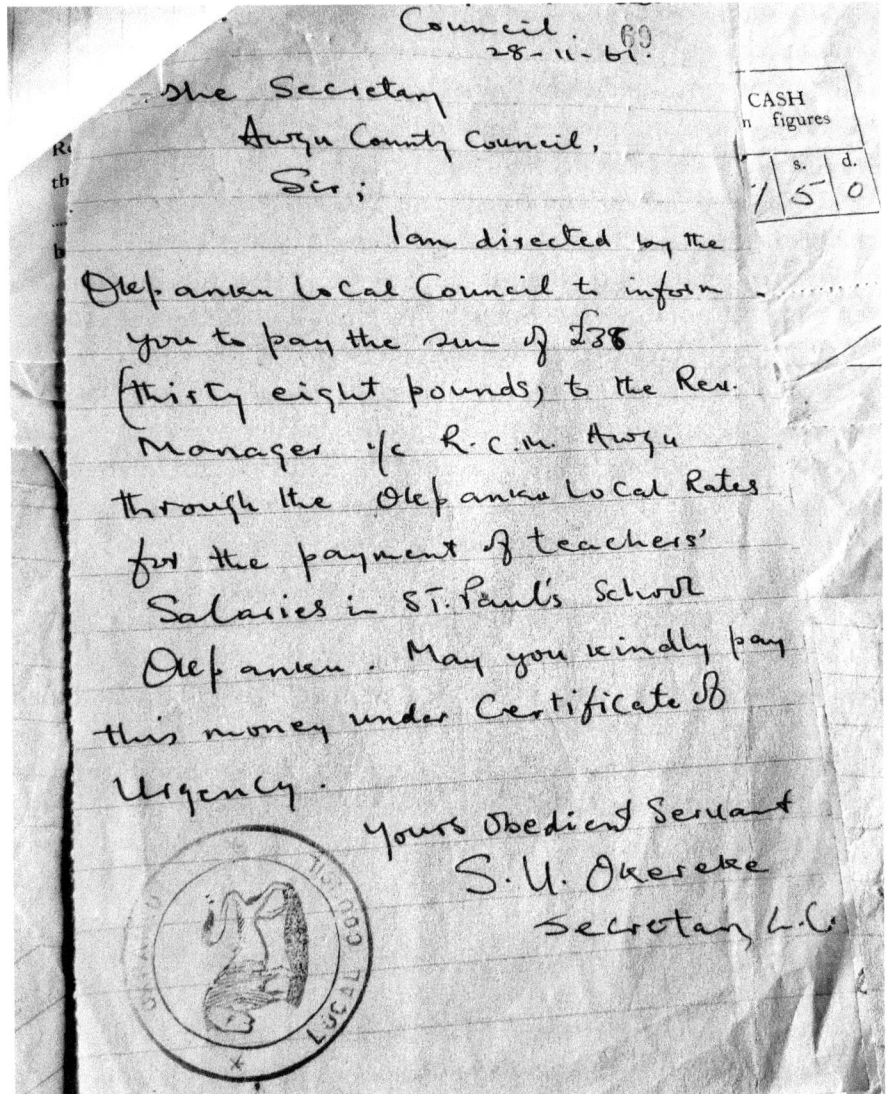

A letter about the Assumed Local Contributions by the author when he was secretary of Okpanku Local Council in 1961.

the infrastructure in our schools. Having served as divisional councilor in Okpanku and in the local council and used communal labor to achieve a lot, I knew what was possible when the people came

． ． ． ． ． ．

together with one mind and spirit. I sold this idea to the rest of the committee and the community. Soon after, we built a five-classroom block and renovated the five-classroom building at Okpanku High School, Amaogudu, which they handed over to the Okpanku community. We also built a school library, science laboratory, staff room, and principal's office, and enlisted an NGO to donate science equipment to the school. Using the experience of when auxiliary teachers were employed by the missionaries to help run the schools, I employed community members as teachers and placed them under the payroll of the Parent Teacher Association.

Social clubs were also formed to help promote peace in the community. It was figured that these clubs would have bylaws to regulate the activities of their members. I was elected vice chairman of Ezienyi Social Club '30 of Nigeria. It was the first club in Okpanku. This was followed shortly by Madu-ka-Ego Social Club of Nigeria, where I have served as chairman since 1986.

These social clubs made headway in controlling court litigations. We believed that residents of Okpanku should be their brothers' keepers and that matters should first be reported to the clubs and community before being taken to court. The bylaws of these clubs helped to promote decent behavior in the community, including controlling sexual harassment. They encouraged education and awarded scholarships to students.

Becoming a Customary Court Judge

New reforms introduced a law abolishing native courts. Nenwe and Oduma were given a separate court, while Mpu, Okpanku, and Ndeaboh remained under one jurisdiction. In 1992, with the creation of these two new courts, now under Enugu State, advertisements were made for the recruitment of customary court judges. My brother, Louis, who was by then a high court judge in Enugu State, advised that I apply. By then, I had familiarized myself with the customs, cultures, and traditions of Okpanku and Igboland in general. I

16. Sojourn into Eze's Court and Customary Court

had served as secretary of Okpanku Local Council for several years and been a member of various social clubs that saw to the development of my community and the entrenchment of good moral values in Okpanku.

From the time I became a teacher and divisional councilor to my time as the secretary of Okpanku Local Council, I gained such experience that I was sure would make me stand out if appointed to the customary court. Written and oral examinations were conducted, and I sailed through. We were then invited for an intensive orientation course.

On October 4, 1993, I was appointed to serve in the customary court. The people of Okpanku and other surrounding communities were excited to learn that I was going to be serving on the court, for at the time, everyone in Okpanku, including children, was aware of my efforts in promoting development and peace in the community. They knew of my experiences in entrenching peace and resolving land and boundary disputes between villages and communities bordering Okpanku.

The customary court was set up, and Chief Emmanuel Ndukwu was the president. I was appointed Member I, while Chief Emmanuel Iteogwu was made Member II. We knew that if we were judicious, we would go down in history as those who worked to promote justice for our people. It was going to be a terrible stain on our reputation if we got mixed up in bribery and corruption. I had become a man known for high integrity and was more than willing to continue to uphold it even as a judge in the customary court. I decided and vowed to be upright and truthful while discharging my duties. I was not going to be bribed, no matter the amount. And this was my guiding principle all through my stay on the customary court, such that there was never an appeal against any judgment we delivered.

One significant case was that between Mr. Anthony Ugwa and the Catholic community of Obu-Ofia Awgu. The president of the Customary Court of Appeal, Enugu, transferred this case to our court after it was tried at the Awgu customary court and the members of that court were found to be biased.

· · · · · ·

After the parties and witnesses had testified before us, we went to Awgu to inspect the land. I insisted on our members being shown the ancient landmarks that were used to mark the boundary of the land by the first Christians when the land was given to them by the locals. The court thereafter discovered that the defendant, Mr. Ugwa, had removed these landmarks and built a fence beyond the boundary. We also noticed other obvious discrepancies. The court gave judgment in favor of the Catholic community, ordered the demolition of the fence, and awarded damages against the defendant. The defendant accepted the judgment and did not appeal it. This attracted the attention of the president of the Customary Court of Appeal, Enugu, who assigned two more such cases to us, one from each of the Awgu and Nenwe customary courts.

It was a great experience, and I owe a lot of thanks to the then registrar of the court, Mr. Anthony Nwankwo, for guiding us on the laws and rules of court and proceedings.

Second Term as a Customary Court Judge

As the end of our tenure drew closer, people showed eagerness to take over our seats. But the locals also loved the way we served. I had served for three years without a stain of bribery. All matters from Okpanku, including divorce, land, taxation, and rates, had been handled and dispatched with care.

Three people from Okpanku indicated interest in my position. We faced written and oral examinations, which I passed with credit. We were given orientation by the chief judge of Enugu State and given appointment letters on March 3, 1997. The new formation of the court was:

Chief Sylvester Okereke—President—Okpanku community
Chief Alexander Osita—Member I—Ndeaboh community
Chief Paul O. Mba—Member II—Mpu community
Mr. Sunday Ogbodo was the court registrar.

· · · · · ·

16. Sojourn into Eze's Court and Customary Court

News spread that I had been made president of the customary court, and many land, divorce, and tax cases flooded our court. Good reputation is like wildfire; it travels fast and consumes everything in its way. I saw that the people of the three communities under the court had placed their trust in me, and as I always did while serving, I made sure to not disappoint them.

Third Term in the Customary Court

On March 31, 2014, our tenure at the customary court ended, and I applied to be re-engaged. The Enugu State government had by then created more courts to serve the people and bring justice closer to them. A court had been set up to serve only Okpanku and Ekoli communities. For my position, there were four aspirants from the two communities. There was a new rule that lawyers were to serve as presidents of the customary courts, and lawyers were now allowed to represent their clients in customary courts. After our examination and appointment, the following were admitted as members of the court:

> Barrister Simon O. Aja—President—Okpanku community
> Chief Sylvester U. Okereke—Member I—Okpanku community
> Chief Augustine O. Chukwu—Member II—Ekoli community
> Mr. Fredrick Igwe was the court registrar, and there were two other members of staff.

We reopened by reviewing outstanding cases before the court, including civil and criminal cases. The court faced challenges, including the unavailability of a full-time court bailiff, for the registrar also served as bailiff. There was also no security or personnel in court to accompany convicts to Orji Prison after trial, so the court applied to Enugu for a police escort. Worse, there were no court papers or books since only the president, who was a lawyer, had books for reference purposes.

We realized that lawyers, now allowed to represent their clients

······

in courts, employed all forms of shenanigans to delay and adjourn cases. Sometimes, they ignored the customs of the people in making their case. Our court adjudicated over more land disputes than divorce and marriage cases, making those lawyers who did not know about the laws of the land rely on their law books and reports, which were not suited for most of the cases.

Despite these challenges, it was a great time and experience for me as I learned a lot from the lawyers and from the president of the court, especially in the areas of jurisprudence. I was encouraged by my position as a member of the customary court to hold myself in high esteem in the society. I always dressed neatly and formally, even while at home. At public functions, I did not partake in entertainment openly. I learned to be punctual and to not have any association with people whose cases were before my court. I ensured that I avoided intervening in matters of dispute in my village or community as such matters might come up before my court. In the king's palace, my advice and experience were sought in handling various cases. I bought law and court books to enrich myself, and this encouraged me to read regularly and broaden my knowledge. I also learned from workshops that were made available to us as members of the customary court.

17

My Philosophy of Life and Religion

Several times, I have been asked about my role models and about what my life motivation is. This is a question that I do not find difficult to answer, and I do not need to second-guess my response.

All my life, I have been inspired by the kind of life my father lived. Okereke Abara's life was an "open book." His life was one of integrity and transparency. He liked to distinguish himself in anything and everything he did and in all projects he embarked on. He was the leader of the hunters' association in Okpanku and discharged his duties steadfastly such that he was well respected.

As a young man and until his dying days, he was determined to ensure that he raised a family of respected statesmen, so he sent his relatives to school and encouraged them to pursue the White man's education without any prompting. When they failed to do this, he ensured that I went to school and did everything possible to ensure that I remained in school, no matter the odds.

Therefore, I always wanted to please and make my father proud. I knew that any wrong step I took would bring shame to his hard-earned reputation. This made me strive to distinguish myself among my peers. At school, I worked hard to make him proud because I knew that there was no room for failure. If my father and his father before him were great hunters and wrestlers and farmers, then it was important that I did better in the fields of teaching and farming and trading in which I found myself.

I also took over the mantle of leadership of the Okereke Abara family and worked hard to care for the family, not only my wife and

The Teacher Boy

The author and his wife, Patricia Okereke, with their six children, left to right: Nneka, Chukwumerije, Amauche, Gregory, Ifeyinwa and Celestine.

children but also my siblings, my father's wives, and my extended family. This responsibility came to rest on my shoulders as soon as I became a young teacher and made me work harder.

Before Christianity came into Okpanku, our people practiced and believed in some deities such as Ali, the earth goddess; Agwu; Ezebinagu; and Ivo Nne Mmini, a strong female deity living in the river. They respected, worshipped, and honored these gods. This was long before Warrant Chief Aja Ngwute traveled to Uturu through Ishiagu with some of the early converts to Christianity to request the European missionaries to set up a church and school at Okpanku. But shortly after, the Reverend Father Trech came to Okpanku and established a church and school, and from then on, Okpanku people embraced Christianity and the religion grew immensely.

Like every Okpanku child who was in school, my first encounter with Christianity was at St. Paul's Catholic School, Okpanku, for it was the norm to learn both religion and the word of God together

· · · · · ·

17. My Philosophy of Life and Religion

with how to read and write. Gradually, these teachings began to appeal to my young mind and took root when I was in St. George's Catholic School, Ndeaboh, as a Standard III pupil. There, we received catechism classes, and I took the name Sylvester at baptism.

From 1948 onwards, I became a changed person. It dawned on me that this new religion, which brought along Western education and gave us the power to read what was written on paper, had other functionalities. In catechism, we wrapped our minds around the concepts of God and God's creation. We learned about our role in life and fate and faith. I realized that faith, just as the catechism teaches, is the spiritual gift that God gives His people, enabling us to believe in Him and in His words and teachings. I began to deepen my faith and trust in Him. I realized from that young age that God was everywhere, could see everything I did as a mortal, and would reward my efforts both here on Earth and in the afterlife.

The awareness that God's rewards for me are limitless and that I can get them both on Earth and in the afterlife, combined with my father's teachings and exemplary life, formed me into the man I am today. My father was a man who valued and respected others while selflessly serving his community. Every day, I strive to be like him by working for my community, my people, and God's people, knowing that my calling is to duty and service despite the difficulties, and often the lack of rewards, appreciation, and thanks. My faith in God and His teachings taught me that for every evil I perform, there is a penalty waiting for me, and that my children could share in it, just as they would from the rewards of any good I do on earth. As a result, I worked hard every day to do justice to people, be fair to them, and carry out my responsibilities with love and empathy.

Sometimes, I have been asked why my life is interwoven into the fabric of Okpanku political and religious history, for the story of Okpanku will never be complete without a mention of my contributions, whether in politics as a divisional councilor, secretary of Okpanku Local Council, customary court judge, or cultural promoter, especially at the Eze's cabinet; or in the church as a catechist and promoter of faith; or in my professional life as a teacher, trader,

· · · · · ·

The Teacher Boy

The author and his wife, Patricia Okereke, with Cardinal John Onaiyekan during their visit to the USA.

and farmer. My answer is always that I learned from my father and from the teachings of God that we are all created with different gifts, and these gifts must be discharged with steadfastness. I realized that my calling was to the service of God's people and that if I failed in it, I had failed in life.

In January 1958, 10 years after I became a full-fledged Catholic by receiving the sacrament of baptism, I was made a catechist. It was not because there were no other people who could read and write at the time or understood the Bible but because it was seen that I was drawn and devoted to God. My life as a catechist from 1958 to 1964 made me a different person. Other politicians could take bribes and treat their people with disdain, but I could not, for I was now like a performer dancing in the market square. All eyes were focused on me. I had to live every day dedicated to the things of God, ensuring that I lived up to what I preached in church. This was why many

・・・・・・

17. My Philosophy of Life and Religion

people came to me to sponsor them, not just in baptism but also in marriage. As a catechist, I sponsored a total of 15 couples in the sacrament of matrimony and 35 persons in the sacrament of baptism and confirmation. After I left office as a catechist, I sponsored four more couples in the sacrament of matrimony. Years later, I still sponsored more than 50 children for infant and adult baptism, 20 for the sacrament of confirmation, and more than 12 couples for the sacrament of matrimony.

I consider the creation of a parish at Okpanku to be one of my crowning achievements, for I championed the project for St. Paul's Catholic Church to become a parish. At the time, our churches in Okpanku, Mpu, and Ezaa Mpu were Catholic stations under St. Michael's Catholic Church, Awgu, since the creation of the Awgu Parish in 1948. The distance from Okpanku to Awgu was over 20 miles, and no one attempted to go there for Holy Mass except on rare occasions. So, if the priest could not come to celebrate Holy Mass at the station, which was often, the catechist led the Mass. It continued like this for many years.

In 1986, a couple who were members of the Assemblies of God Mission held their wedding service inside St. Paul's Catholic Church, Okpanku, against all resistance and admonitions. This couple claimed that the church building was owned by every member of the community since it was built by Okpanku people under communal labor. I resisted this move, to no avail, and warned them in writing through their reverend pastor not to try such a thing again.

Years later in August 1995, some youths staged a football match on the premises of St. Paul's Church while the Reverend Father Cyprian Oji was celebrating the Holy Mass. This caused a riot between members of the church and the youths. Thereafter, the chairman of Okpanku Youth Movement at the time, being an adherent of Assemblies of God Mission, began to make moves to convert St. Paul's Church and School into a community secondary school. I put up a strong resistance against this move and halted it. I was the chairman of the Christian Men Association of the churches in Okpanku, Mpu, and Ezaa Mpu at the time. I petitioned the governor

The Teacher Boy

of Enugu State, the State Criminal Investigation Department at Enugu, the district police officer of Awgu, the reverend father in Awgu, the bishop of Enugu Diocese, Bishop Michael Eneje, the eze of Okpanku, and the chairman of Awgu Local Government Council.

The bishop set up a committee consisting of Monsignor Okpara Ibekwe; the Reverend Father Adike, who was the parish priest of Awgu Parish; HRH R. A. Chukwu and his cabinet; and police representatives, while I was the spokesperson for the Catholic church. After hearing from me and the other interested parties, including the youths and members of Assemblies of God Mission, a decision was reached that the land and its property belonged to the Catholic Church, not minding who contributed to its labor, and no individual or group was allowed to trespass into it.

On August 6, 1993, under my leadership, Monsignor Luke Adike laid the foundation stone for a parsonage on the land. I had already gotten the church's land surveyed that same year. My efforts for the growth of the Catholic Church in Okpanku and neighboring communities are testaments known to people today, as I chaired several committees for the church building and for the ordination of priests.

In all, I have continued to believe and practice the teachings of God and the Church. During the early days, Christians were seen as the enemies of pagans. Those who practiced the African traditional religion did not give out their wards in marriage to Christians, and vice versa. Christians did not attend any funeral organized by traditionalists. In Okpanku, it is customary that when one's father dies, a cow must be killed in his honor. Some Christians at the time opposed this practice and refused to do it. But I believe that since the cow is not sacrificed to any idol at the funeral but killed for family members in the honor of the deceased, that it has not gone against the teachings and doctrines of the Church. When my father passed, I killed a cow to honor him.

At the peak of the segregation between Christians and traditionalists, I established the Umunna meetings for men and women of the Umuogudu family as a way of uniting us and ensuring lasting

······

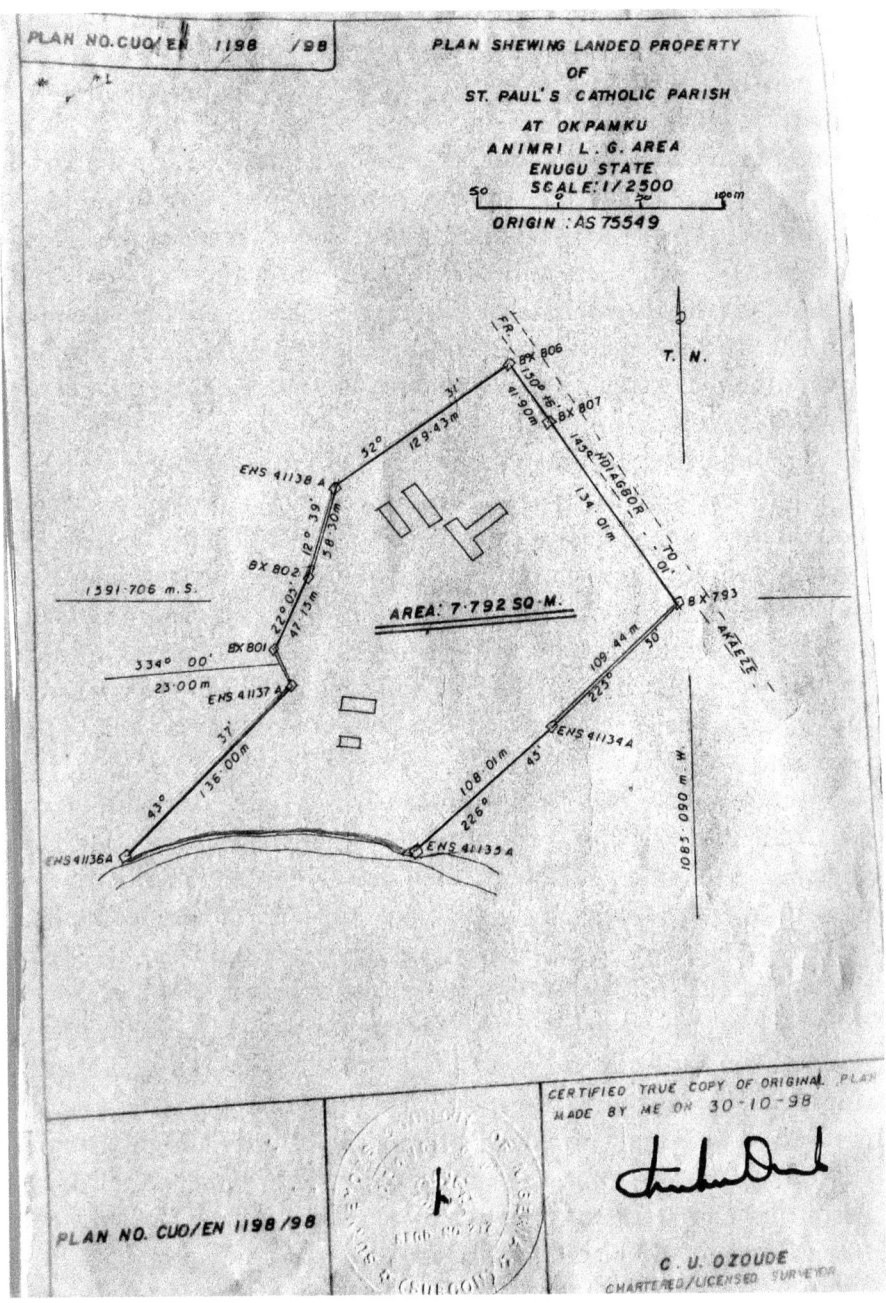

A surveyor's plan showing the land that belongs to St. Paul's Parish, Okpanku, kept in custody by the author since 1998.

The Teacher Boy

peace without regard to anyone's religious beliefs or affiliations. I initiated and encouraged workshops, seminars, and lectures for both adherents to educate everyone on respect for the other's beliefs and practices. This ensured that Christians stopped destroying idols and buildings housing them, and traditionalists learned that those idols are not God. These efforts helped to convert many pagans and encouraged the growth of Christianity. All members of my extended family and kindred converted to Christianity, including my father and mother before they passed. My mother was baptized while in her nineties.

Looking back now at my life and activities, I do not see service to humanity as a struggle. There is never a moment of indecision on my part in choosing public service that benefits my people. And this is why I feel embittered when I watch public servants of today. I see that today, people's attitudes toward service and leadership have changed. During our time, the reward was the respect and honor one got from his people and society. Today, the reward is materialism, the eagerness to enrich oneself to the detriment of the people.

But I have learned lessons in my life as a public servant. I have learned that leaders mostly do not know what people say about them and their behavior until they leave office. A leader will not always be spoken well of by everybody, but a majority of the people can recognize and know if the leader is good or not and will surely pay the leader back with greater opportunities to serve and in many other ways. One example is the decision of my people that I represent them for a second term as divisional councilor and then a third. Another is the decision recently by the Enugu State government to make Amaeze an autonomous community and my people, without prompting, coming to inform me that I would be their king. Also, I have not been changed as a member of the Eze's cabinet since 1996. I was always also encouraged to serve as a customary court judge.

There have been times when I was tempted to receive a bribe or go against the teachings of God and my conscience. As a customary

・・・・・・

17. My Philosophy of Life and Religion

court judge, I can recall at least three times when people approached me with bribes. There was a time when a woman was in court over a land case. One of the parties came to me with a large sum of money, which I rejected. After I gave judgment, the party who tried to bribe me came to thank and praise me and said that even though I refused to accept their money to give judgment in their favor, they had immense respect for me.

I am now 86 years old and have seen the world and experienced life. I believe that leaders must be obedient to the people, for without the people they are nothing, without the people they serve no one. A leader must be dedicated to their duty and must go about it with humility. It is shameful and disappointing to see today's leaders strut and behave as if they are the leaders of themselves.

I will not forget Chiefs Lawrence A. Ukpai, P. O. Mbah from Mpu, and G. U. Achi, who were my political mentors. I remember them very fondly. When I lost my first wife, Chief G. U. Achi was among the people who continuously advised and encouraged me. His words of encouragement helped me to survive the ordeal. He was a headmaster of my school at the time and was also the one who encouraged me to serve as a divisional councilor when I was approached by the community to do so. He told me that in his place the position was highly contestable.

Chief Lawrence A. Ukpai was helpful, and his wisdom and advice helped to shape me as a politician. He was the paramount chief of Okpanku who was co-opted into the council, and we worked together, along with Mr. Jeremiah Obasi, at the county council. I have immense respect for him.

Chief Ukpai and I went for teacher training together. I fondly remember an incident that happened after we resumed work. We were living together as teachers at the time and had worked for three months without payment. The day we were paid, Chief Ukpai brought out his salary and spread it on the floor. He asked me to get two sticks and also spread my money on the floor. He began to beat the cash spread on the floor with one of the sticks, and I followed suit with the other.

・・・・・・

The Teacher Boy

"Money, you think you are stronger than me? Now, I am beating you. Can you see that after you made me go hungry for months, I can beat you now?"

He was a man who had a great sense of humor.

18

Family Is Everything

It was Mario Puzo who wrote that friendship is almost the equal of family. This means that Mario Puzo himself understood that there is nothing greater than family. My father understood this more than his contemporaries and worked all his life to see his family grow, not just in size but in wealth and status. At his time, a man was respected and honored based on the number of wives he had, and Okereke Abara married four. A man's worth was also measured by his number of children, and my father had 12. A man was also measured by the size of his yam barn, and Okereke Abara was a known farmer who took the highest yam chieftaincy title of *Ikeohu*. All these were to ensure that the Abara Okereke family was respected in Okpanku and beyond.

When my father saw that Western education was another achievement that bestowed respect and honors on a man, he worked hard to ensure that his own family got that education. He sent his cousin, Okereke Aja Nwaigbo; his half-brother, Okereke Joseph Ogbonna; and his nephew, Abara Ugo, to school. Unfortunately, none of them saw the value in education. While he was a visionary, they were shortsighted and all dropped out, causing him a heartbreak that he never ceased talking about. My father, Okereke Abara, then decided to send me to school. I was his son, after all, and he figured that I would not disobey him. I recall seeing the glimmer in his eyes the day I graduated from Standard VI and became an educated man at the time and subsequently when I became a teacher. It is difficult to put into words how he felt the day I became a divisional councilor and when I was made a catechist, though he was not a Christian at the time.

······

The author and his wife, Patricia Okereke, with a Catholic cardinal during their visit to the USA.

All of this points to a man who held family in high esteem and believed in it. Before my father passed, he made me promise him not to abandon our family. I promised to care for my brother, my stepsiblings, and my father's four wives. It was not an easy task, being a boy myself who had to do this with the little remuneration that came from teaching at a primary school, but it was a task from which I did

· · · · · ·

18. Family Is Everything

not waver. Even when I was disengaged from work because I failed to go for further education, I still ensured that my father's wives and their children were well cared for.

Many people saw how I toiled to farm tens of acres of land and laughed behind my back, saying I was going to die someday from hard labor, but I was not deterred, for there was no one else to feed the numerous mouths waiting for me at home. I divided the land my father left for us among his four wives and still gave them the funds to farm on their portion. After harvest, I also made sure they got food from my farms as well. I paid for their children's education and sponsored those who did not want to go to school in various trade and skill acquisition programs.

The responsibility for their survival during the civil war fell on my shoulders. During that war, I had not only my wife and little children to care for but also my extended family. I knew that those who died during the war did not receive honorable burial and funeral, and I did not want any of my family to suffer this fate.

After this, I gave every male member of my family accommodation in my home until they got married and could afford to have a house of their own. I also contributed morally and financially toward their marriages. Most importantly, I had immense love for my siblings, like Louis, whom I trained in school and helped secure two scholarships as a divisional councilor. He retired years later as a judge of the Enugu High Court, and whenever I remember where he is now in society and the status he has achieved, I feel pleased that I made that decision, years ago, to send him to college.

My Lovely Children

Today, I believe God rewarded all the efforts I made in providing for my father's family by giving me six wonderful, trusted, loving, and talented children. They are Nneka Bridget Okereke, Engr. (Dr.) Gregory U. Okereke, Mr. Celestine O. Okereke, Prof. Chukwumerije Okereke, Mrs. Francisca Ifeyinwa Okereke Uzonu, and Mrs.

• • • • • •

The Teacher Boy

Stella Amauche Okereke Anene. My children have all surpassed me in education, and their achievements dwarf mine in so many ways. I was raised by a father who made me his friend and had conversations with me in times of challenges, while at the time, parents gave orders to their children, who had no option but to follow blindly. This has encouraged me to raise children who think freely and creatively. I do not give advice to my children separately but strive to ensure that they listen to my advice as one and learn from my life's examples, successes, and mistakes.

I have based my spiritual teachings to my children on such biblical verses as Romans 12:6, which says that God has given us different gifts for doing certain things well. I encourage them to not ever pretend to love others but to really love

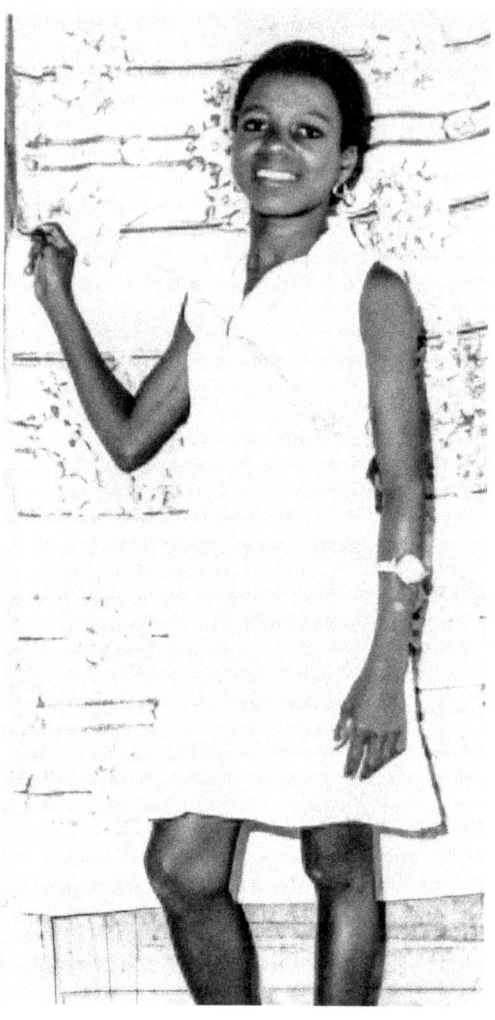

Nneka Okereke, the first daughter of the author, during her days in secondary school.

them and to hate what is wrong and to hold tightly to what is good. I raised my children never to be lazy but to work hard and serve the Lord enthusiastically. I educated them to be patient in trouble and to always pray, and to not let evil conquer them but to conquer evil by doing good.

· · · · · ·

18. Family Is Everything

I teach and see my children practice what I teach them. Before I got married and while raising my children, I always loved the teachings in Romans 8:27–29, which says that we know that God causes everything to work together for the good of those who love Him and are called according to His purpose. This has been my inspiration.

Having been married for decades now, I know that marriage is about making mistakes and accepting these mistakes to make amends. It is knowing that we are all fallible and yet still committing to spend the rest of our life with that somebody we chose from the beginning while making milk that nurtures and sustains the union.

After the loss of my first wife, Virginia, in 1958, I knelt in prayers to God, morning and night, asking for His mercy. One day, in a vision, I read Revelation 22:12, which says that God is coming soon, bringing His reward with Him to repay all people according to their deeds. I opened my eyes and was amazed that the scripture I had read was in a vision. Shortly after, my heart melted for a girl in my class. When I saw her, I knew God had shown her to me to be my life partner. I would have lost her when I dropped her ambition to further her education at St. Joseph's Teacher Training College, Aba, for that of my brother Louis Okereke, but God had destined that she would be my wife.

My wife, Patricia, is a woman of immense natural wisdom and intelligence. She has done for me, in many ways, more than what Josephine did for Napoleon. I feel very lucky every day to have met her, especially when I see that though we are in our old age now, we remain ever fond of each other. When I look into her eyes, I see the love she has for me, and it pleases me to know that this love has not dwindled or withered all these many years.

Through Patricia, my wife, God rewarded me with children who care for me and are now the source of my life. They are the reason why, at 86, I am hale and hearty and look 50. They maintain and replenish my bank account, maintain my car, pay my driver, and provide for my household and for my upkeep.

In 2017, my daughter Nneka Okereke took my wife and me on a trip to the United States of America, where she resides. We boarded a

The Teacher Boy

The author and his wife, Patricia Okereke, during their visit to the United States of America.

flight from the Akanu Ibiam International Airport, Enugu; picked up connecting flights in Ethiopia and Dublin; and arrived in the United States by 1:00 p.m. on May 5, 2017.

It was a surreal and amazing experience for me, not least beacuse I had become the first in the entire Okpanku to be taken to America and the UK by my children. Who would have thought or believed that the teacher boy, the boy from Amaeze Okpanku who played and danced *odabara* and *une* in the village square and lived in a forest during the civil war while war planes crisscrossed the skies and machine gun sounds made people pee in their pants, would traverse the nooks and crannies of America and the UK? Astonishingly,

· · · · · ·

18. Family Is Everything

while in America, I was appointed a member of the Montgomery County Circuit Court to serve from 2017 to 2019. It was as if my chi had whispered to them that I once served in the customary court in Nigeria. I could only imagine how my father would be feeling in the great beyond, knowing that I was appointed to serve in the court of the White men in whose native courts in Nigeria he had had experiences that created the unquenchable fire in him to see everyone around him, especially me, get education.

In the United States we visited Nneka's office at the World Bank Headquarters in Washington, D.C., where I was proud to learn she was the team leader in her department. I would not have imagined that my daughter would work with Americans and people of other races and have them receive orders from her. She took me to have a close look at the White House and the Capitol Building. My wife and I were thrilled to visit the Red Cross headquarters, which I was eager to see, owing to the good work they did for the Igbos during the Biafran War. We visited and saw the Museum for African Arts, the Nigerian Embassy, the National Air and Space Museum, and many other revered places in United States capital, Washington, D.C. During this visit, which lasted for seven months, my daughter held a big party in honor of my 80th birthday. My son, Professor Chukwumerije, flew in from the UK with his family for this party, which they held as a surprise. My joy knew no bounds, as my wife and I were ushered into the party hall full of Nigerians, Americans, and other nationals who were my daughter's friends, colleagues, and neighbors in America. It was during my time in the United States that I began to write this story.

On November 24, 2017, we left the US and arrived in the UK, where my son Professor Chukwumerije Okereke lives with his family. My son Chukwumerije is today a professor of global repute who has affiliation with several universities including the London School of Economics; the University of Bristol, UK; Alex Ekwueme Federal University, Nigeria; and the world-famous University of Oxford, UK. During my visit to the UK, my professor son took us to see the Houses of Parliament in London, Westminster Abbey, and the Westminster Bridge. I was also delighted to see the statue of Winston Churchill,

······

Author, wife and grandchildren during a visit to Trafalgar Square, London, in December 2017. From left to right: Chioma, author, Patricia (wife), and Chukwuebuka.

18. Family Is Everything

Author, wife, daughter-in-law, and grandchildren visiting the Houses of Parliament in London. From left to right: author, Chioma, Chukwuebuka, Boma, Chinemerem, and Patricia (wife).

St. James Park, Buckingham Palace, and the Queen's Gallery. I was happy to visit Oxford University, which I consider a home for learning and illumination in the world, and I am now proud that my son is associated with that ancient and most prestigious university. We also visited the University of Reading, where Prof. Okereke was working at the time.

Now, when asked what I can show for all these many years of sacrifice and hard work for my people, I remember my children and smile in satisfaction.

· · · · · ·

Index

Aaron, Arum 40
Abara, Ivo Chukwu 44
Abara, Okereke 13, 15, 16, 17, 19, 37, 43, 44, 45, 46, 47, 49, 57, 65, 68, 84, 88, 112, 161, 171
Abara, Onwukwe Onu 41
Abara, Ugo 37, 171
Abiriba 22
Abochi, Bernard 69
Abraham Ajaegwu 100, 101, 135
Abubakar Tafawa Balewa (Sir) 105
Achebe, Chinua 31, 134
Achi, Alice 77
Achi, G.U. (chief) 169
Adike, Luke (Monsignor) 166
Adike, the Rev. Fr. 166
affluence 16
Afikpo 44, 46, 82, 128, 130, 131
Afor Market Day 20, 63, 121
*African Morning Po*st 13
African traditional religion 166
Agbakara 22
Agwu, Francis O. 72, 149
Aja, Alexander 20
Aja, Chukwu 125
Aja, Cyprian 139
Aja, Dike 42
Aja, Elewe 91
Aja Elewe, Okoro 41
Aja, Elias 39
Aja, Fredrick 125
Aja, Makwe 48
Aja, Mathew 48
Aja, Nwachukwu 99
Aja, Okereke 37, 105, 171
Aja, Paul 148
Aja, Peter 38, 39, 40
Aja, Simon 35, 39, 41
Aja, Simon O. (Bar) 159
Ajah, Oshi 62, 63
Ajali, Choke 127
Ajanne Uka, Donald 64
Ajaonu, Paul 40

Ajofia 11, 40, 126
Akaeze Community 18, 46, 76, 103, 127, 131, 135, 150, 154
Akanu Ibiam International Airport 176
Akata, Stephen 95
Akpa, Edmund 65, 68
Akpa, Makwe 46
Akpakoro 53
Akwa eriri 55
Alex Ekwueme Federal University 177
Alfred, Chukwu 52
Aliebo Amaogudu 34
Aliewu, Obasi 135
Amabiriba Central School 150
Amabiriba Village 22, 34, 43, 52, 85, 108, 130, 152
Amachalla Mpu 69
Amaeze Village 34, 35
Amagu Village 34, 35, 149
Amaogudu Village 34, 35, 149
Amasiri 128
Anene, Stella Amauche 174
Anglo-Aro War 6, 32
Ani, Augustine Igwe (HRH) 145
Aninri Local Government Council 151
Anthony, Chukwu Ukpai 140
Anya, Benjamin 70
Anyata, Eugene 64
Anyim, Edwin 70
Anyim, Juliana 111
Aroh, Edwin O. 72, 149
Arochukwu 32, 39, 40, 130, 134
Arrow of God 31
auxiliary teachers 42, 43, 67, 70, 97, 116, 156
Avu Atu Egwu 18
Awgu County Council Secondary School, Nenwe 97, 141
Awgu Customary Court 157
Awgu Divisional Council 43, 85, 149, 153
Awgu Parish 165
Awolowo, Obafemi (chief) 137
Azi, Ogbonna 59

· · · · · ·

181

Azikiwe, Nnamdi 13
Azimkpari, Christian 112
Azionu, Ejiaka 51
Azu-nkwo 52
Azuokwu, Edwin 126

barn 16, 17, 38, 47, 74, 102, 109, 171
Bello, Ahmadu (Sir) 105
Biafran 5, 95, 129, 130, 131, 132, 133, 134, 135, 136, 137, 177
blood covenant 25
British Broadcasting Corporation (BBC) 135
Buckingham Palace 179
Buckley, the Rev. Fr. T. 115, 127

Capitol Building, Washington, DC 117
cassava cultivation 22, 120
catechist 7, 9, 82, 96, 107, 111, 127, 163, 164, 165, 171
chief judge of Enugu State 158
chieftaincy rites 12
Chime Nkwo, Sololon Eze (HRH) 99
China-Japan War 13
Chukwu, Augustine O. (chief) 159
Chukwu, Daniel 149
Chukwu, Ezekiel (chief) 105
Chukwu, Festus O. (HRH) 150, 154
Chukwu, Mathias 102
Chukwu, Ogwo 19, 47
Chukwu, Peter 97
Chukwu, Reginald R. (HRH) 166
Chukwueze, Gabriel 36
Chukwurah, Mark 77, 115
Chuma, Ogwo 46
Churchill, Winston 177
climate change 2, 22
Cocoyam 18, 110, 132
Coleman, the Rev. Father 62
Community Primary School, Amaeze Okpanku 147
Corpus Christi College, Achi 97, 112, 114, 117
customary courts 148, 158, 159; judges 7, 148, 152, 156, 158, 163, 168

dancing troupes 20
deity 30, 162
Dibia, Onuoha 51
Dimgba 18
disengaged from work 117
Disney, Walt 13
divisional councilor 42, 82, 85, 86, 87, 89, 91, 93, 94, 95, 97, 98, 99, 101, 103, 105, 107, 111, 129, 135, 137, 141, 142, 152, 155, 157, 163, 168, 169, 171, 173
Dublin 176
Dumoke 119

Eastern Railway Line 148
Ebonyi State 20, 54, 95, 99
eclipse of the sun 12
Ede 39
Effiong, Phillip (Col.) 136
Egunkwo 100
Eke, Chukwu 99
Ekoli community 159
Elechi, Christopher 123
Elizabeth II (Queen) 73, 179
Enebe, Tobias 54
Eneje, Michael (Bishop) 166
Enugu High Court 103, 173
Enugu State 15, 40, 92, 156, 158, 159, 166, 168
Eru, Chukwu 125
Ethiopia 176
Europe 1, 12, 37
European missionaries 15, 22, 25, 44, 58, 162
Evil Forest 11, 19, 110
Ewo, Janet 111
Ezaa Mpu 165
Eze, Charles 145
Eze, Cosmas 89
Eze, Emmanuel 96, 145
Eze, Ivo 19
Eze Nwabo, Sunday 55, 56
Eze Oha I of Okpanku 150
Ezekiel, Chienye 100
Ezeoke, Kalu 127
Ezeulu 31
Ezi-enyi Social Club 156

fathers 2, 12, 37, 38, 57, 60
fattening rooms 12, 28
festivals 3, 12, 15, 26, 27, 29, 31, 76, 152; *Ibu-anu* 27, 78; *Ijiegbe* 24, 28, 29, 55, 57, 58, 59, 60, 61, 63, 64, 68, 74, 78; *Ikeji* 24, 26, 29, 122; *Ikeohu* 22, 23, 171; *Inwuegbe* 27, 57; *Inye ive la eka* 26, 78; *Omoha* 24, 26, 31, 76
firewood 47, 56, 63
First School Leaving Certificate examinations 64

Gibbs, Mr. 124, 125
goat keeping 12, 133
gods 12, 30, 70, 162
Gold Coast 13
Gowon, Gen. Yakubu 129, 130, 136, 137
Grade II teacher 143, 147
gunpowder 62, 63

harvest 22, 31, 68, 76, 82, 122, 132, 137, 173
Hitchcock, Dr. William 1, 32
Holy Ghost congregation 35

Index

Holy Rosary College, Enugu 143
Houses of Parliament in London 177
hunter 17, 32, 37, 44, 62, 83, 100, 161
hunting of games 17, 20, 23, 47, 48, 50, 100
hut, living inside 17, 23, 24, 38, 39, 52

Ibe, Nwa Makwe 40
Ibekwe, Okpara (Monsignor) 166
Ifeajuna, Emmanuel (Major) 105
Igwe, Fredrick 159
Igwebuike Age-grade 20
Ihuibe Village 34, 35, 135, 149
Ije, Cyprian Igwe (HRH) 145
Iloka, E. (Hon) 89
intertribal war 25
Ironsi, Aguiyi (General) 105, 106
Ishiagu 30, 33, 34, 44, 46, 57, 59, 60, 61, 62, 63, 64, 72, 76, 97, 124, 162
Isiukwuato 100
Itata, Ogbu Chukwu (chief) 88
Itata, Ogbu Chukwu (Mazi) 126, 127
Iteogwu, Emmanuel (chief) 157
Ituku 72
Ivo, Una 19
Ivo Bridge 81, 94, 101, 134, 150
Ivo Oti, Ivo Rebecca 111
Ivo River 1, 18, 19, 55, 94, 150
Ivoke, Aja Eze (Lance Corporal) 39
Ivoke, Ambrose 150
Ivoke, Paul 39, 125
Ivoke, Theresa 71
Ivory Coast (Côte d'Ivoire) 136

Japan 13
Josephine (wife of Napoleon) 175

Kama, Fidelis 69
kinsmen 95, 119, 120
kola nuts 30, 122, 127

Lewis, C.S. 80
London School of Economics 2, 177

Madu-ka-Ego Social Club of Nigeria 156
Makwe, Dick 125
Makwe, Onu 72
Makwe, Ukpai 134, 135
manhood rites 5, 12, 58
Mazi Inyinya 16, 122
Mazi title 74
Mba, Duke 89
Mba, Paul O. (chief)
Mbara, Ogbo 53
Mbubu, Innocent 137, 139
McGreen, Rev. Fr. 43, 53, 67, 70, 71, 87, 116
Metu, B.I. (Bar.) 103
Mgbomu Okposi 18, 20, 46, 96, 99, 100

Mgborie, Ngwute 52, 53
Mgbowo community 49, 65
missionaries 6, 13, 15, 22, 25, 35, 40, 43, 44, 49, 58, 156, 162
Mkpume Asaa I of Okpanku 151
Montgomery County Circuit Court 177
moonlight dances 1, 19
Moses, Akpaeru 134
Mpu 25, 69, 70, 71, 85, 92, 116, 122, 124, 132, 148, 150, 156, 165, 169
myrrh gum 22

Native Court 5, 34, 35, 44, 57, 90, 91, 99, 148, 156, 177
Ndeaboh Community School 36, 49, 158
Ndeaboh Native Court 91, 148
Ndukwu, Emmanuel (chief) 157
Nenwe Community 69, 92, 97, 141, 148, 156, 158
Ngwoke, Okorie 55
Ngwute, Ajah (Paramount chief) 34, 35, 36, 37, 39, 40, 84, 126
Ngwute, Mgborie 52, 53
Njoku, Chukwu 30, 31, 120
Njoku, Patrick A. 149
Njoku, Ukpai 15, 18, 23, 46, 74
Nso Njoku 30
nudity 12, 19, 58
Nwabo, Eze 55, 56
Nwafor, David 123
Nwaja, Ugo 19
Nwanyi, Ude 112
Nwaonye, Francis 39
Nwaonye, Obi 91
Nwokedi, P.K. (Bar) 103
Nwokpoke, Agada 95
Nwonye, Francis Chukwu 41
Nwosu, Donald 97
Nwururu, Udu 111
Nzeogwu, Chukwuma Kaduna (Major) 105

oaths 15
Obasi, Ferdinand 121
Obasi, Jeremiah (councilor) 35, 41, 42, 85, 86, 89, 91, 124, 149, 164
Obuoma 20, 28
Ochi, G.U. (chief) 40, 72, 89
Odabara 19, 20, 48, 176
Odo 12, 26, 59, 60, 68
Oduma community 92, 124, 130, 148, 156
off liquor license 121
Ofili, Ferdinand 70
Ogbodo, Sunday 158
Ogbonna, Mark 97, 105
Ogbu Chukwu Itata 88, 126, 127
Ogbu Evi 17, 18
Ogbuagu, Jonas (Hon) 145

· · · · · ·

183

Ogbukere Gbusuo Agha 109
Ogo, Ukpani 134
Ogo, Umhai
Ogu, Egbe 40
Ogwo, Chukwu 35
Ogwo, Obasi 20
Ogwo, Obasi (Mazi) 20
Ogwo, Salome 113
Ogwu Aviaekpa 127
Ogwudu, Sunday 132
Ogwumabiri 123
Ogwumabiri Market 121, 154
Ohawgu, Mrs. Comfort 123
Ojengwa, Ignatius O. (chief) 145
Oji, the Rev. Fr. Cyprian 165
Ojiakor, Patrick 87
Ojukwu, Lt. Col. Emeka Odumegwu 136
Okafor, B.I.A. 140
Okeke, Paul 141
Okereke, Abara 15, 18, 44, 119, 171
Okereke, Aja Nwaigbo 37, 171
Okereke, Celestine O. 173
Okereke, Chukwu 105, 126
Okereke, Prof. Chukwumerije 1–10, 29, 71, 133, 162, 177, 178
Okereke, David 126
Okereke, Francisca Ifeyinwa 173
Okereke, Gregory U. Engr. 173
Okereke, Joseph 13, 37
Okereke, Joseph Ogbonna 171
Okereke, Louis 97, 112, 175
Okereke, Nneka Bridget 9, 133, 146, 174, 175, 178
Okereke, Obasi 15, 126
Okigwe 35, 103, 104, 112, 114, 148
Okigwe District Court 148
Okigwe High Court 103, 104
Okorie, C. Patrick 72, 149
Okorie, Johnson 119, 120
Okorie, Joshua 95
Okorie, Patrick C. 72, 149
Okorie, Sylvanus 19, 54, 57
Okorie, Sylvanus Ngwoke 55
Okoro, Damian 70, 145
Okoro, Felix 145
Okoro, Hyacinth 19, 64
Okoro, Paulinus (Stg.) 145
Okoroafor, Moses 149
Okorocha, the Rev. 40
Okpanku community 15, 155, 158, 159
Okpanku High School, Amaogudu 156
Okposi 18, 20, 46, 96, 99, 100
Okposi, Mgbom 99, 100
Okposi community 20
Okpu Village 149
Okwa 27
Onitsha Main Market 140, 142

Onu, John 22, 35, 39
Onu, Michael 20, 105
Onu, Ogidi 126
Onu, Okereke (Mazi)
Onu, Paul Ajah 91
Onyeabor, Simon 144
Onyiba, F.O. 89
orator 17
Orieji, Abara Onu 74
Orieji, Virginia 72, 74
Orji, Chukwu Nwaokoro 48
Orji, Ngagha 121
Orji Prison 159
Orlando, Peter Gunning 148
Oshi 35, 62, 63
Oshi, Felix 70
Osita, Alexander (chief) 158
Osita, Fredrick 144
Oti, Thomas 54
Ovum 70
Owerre-ebu forest 135
Owo, Ukwu (chief) 32, 33, 34
Oxford University 2, 177, 179

pagans 166, 168
palm plantation 8, 122, 124, 128
palm seedling and trees 125, 126, 127, 128
palm wine 3, 17, 26, 49, 50, 56, 65, 74, 88, 127
paramount chief 6, 33, 34, 35, 37, 39, 40, 84, 124, 125, 148, 149, 150, 169
Parent Teacher Association 156
Public Health, Education and Scholarship 89, 92, 96, 116, 141
public service 168

Radio Biafra 135
Radio Nigeria 135
raffia mat 23
rituals 12, 15

Sacrament of Baptism 82, 164, 165
Sacrament of Confirmation 53, 165
Sacrament of Matrimony 165
sacrifice 11, 12, 105, 114, 117, 166, 179
St. Anthony's Catholic School, Ishiagu 57, 60, 62, 64
St. Charles Onitsha 5, 7, 150
St. George's Catholic School, Ndeaboh 49, 50, 51, 52, 163
St. Joseph's Catholic School, Mpu 69, 70, 71
St. Joseph's Teacher Training College, Aba 117, 175
St. Mary's Catholic School, Ihe, 72
St. Michael's Catholic Church, Awgu 67, 69, 77, 114, 139, 165
St. Paul's Catholic Church 36, 41, 82, 87, 96, 165

Index

St. Paul's Catholic School, Okpanku 36, 40, 42, 47, 50, 62, 67, 69, 71, 77, 86, 96, 108, 109, 130, 162, 165, 167
St. Paul's Catholic School, Uburu 57, 61, 62, 64
St. Paul's Teacher Training College, Awka 112, 117, 140
St. Theresa's Catholic School, Amaeze 101, 143
School Based Management Committee 154
Secretary of OLC 96, 153, 155, 157, 163
slave merchants 11
slave trade 11
slavery 11, 25
Snow White and the Seven Dwarfs 13
Sy de Moon 87, 116, 117, 119, 121, 123

Tax Assessment Committee 116
title taking 16
tobacco snuff 79, 140, 142
Trech, the Rev Father 35, 36, 40, 162
twilight 20

Ubani, Makwe 121
Ubeagu 70
Uburu 18, 25, 46, 54, 55, 56, 57, 61, 62, 63, 64, 72, 131, 132
Uburu Joint Hospital 150
Uche, Luke 51
Uche, Vincent 40
Udeobasi, Vincent 143
Udumali 15, 33
Uguru, Nteshi 95
Ugwa, Anthony 157
Uhuezeoke Village 34
Uke 41, 69
Ukoku 24, 29, 38
Ukpabi, Festus 100, 101, 102, 105
Ukpabi, Job 40
Ukpai, Lawrence A. (chief) 42, 125, 126, 140, 149, 150, 169
Umezuruike, Emmanuel 89
Umuajali family 40
Umuchime kindred 20

Umunna meetings 88, 166
Umuogudu Kindred 152, 166
Umurah 53
Una, Ivo 19
Une 19, 20, 48, 176
Uneke 91, 134
Uneke Nwenyi, Uneke (Hon) 99
United States of America 118 155
University of Bristol 10, 177
Uri 12, 26
Ururuka 95
Uturu 35, 162
Uzo, Ada Janet 111
Uzo, Elewe 46
Uzoigwe, Andrew 51
Uzoigwe, D.C. (chief) 151
Uzoigwe, Donatus 145
Uzoigwe, Elewe 17, 19
Uzoigwe, Elijah 40
Uzoigwe, George 39
Uzoigwe, Jacob 100
Uzoigwe, Margaret Udenwanyi 111
Uzoigwe, Mathias 54, 56, 64
Uzoigwe, Ngagha 23, 24
Uzoigwe, Njoku 47
Uzoigwe, Patricia 108, 109, 112, 114
Uzoigwe, Sylvester 3, 13, 89
Uzoigwe, Uneke 91, 134
Uzuekoli 131

village square 19, 20, 47, 48, 58, 135, 176

warrant chief 34, 40, 84, 90, 91, 148, 162
warriors 18, 32, 109
West African pilot 13
Westminster Abbey 177
White House 177
Women Training College, Enugu 147
World Bank 9, 177
World War II 17, 37, 38, 39
wrestling 18, 33, 116

Yam Barn 16, 17, 74, 102, 171
Youth Corp 154

www.ingramcontent.com/pod-product-compliance
Ingram Content Group UK Ltd.
Pitfield, Milton Keynes, MK11 3LW, UK
UKHW021846140426
5217IPUK00022B/1615